Igniting the Spirit at Work

Igniting the Spirit at Work

Daily Reflections

Marilyn Mason, Ph.D.

Hazelden
Center City, Minnesota 55012-0176

1-800-328-0094
1-651-213-4590 (Fax)
www.hazelden.org

Library of Congress Cataloging-in-Publication Data

Mason, Marilyn J.
    Igniting the spirit at work : daily reflections /
Marilyn Mason.
        p.   cm.
    Includes index.
    ISBN 1-56838-741-5 (paperback)
    1. Work—Psychological aspects—Miscellanea.
I. Title.

BF481 .M385 2001
158.1'28—dc21

                                        2001026404

05 04 03 02 01   6 5 4 3 2 1

Cover design by Mary Brucken
Cover illustration by David Moore
Interior design by Rachel Holscher
Typesetting by Stanton Publication Services, Inc.

To those who know we light our paths from within,
and dare to ignite
their spirits . . .
at work. . . .

Introduction

Spiritual flatness is the term I use to describe most of the workplaces I have entered as a consultant and as an employee. All too often we see isolation, fear, cynicism, and insecurity. In this day and age, we are spiritually hungry, and negative conditions at work only add to the hunger. Whether we're conscious of it or not, we long for greater connection, peace of mind, and well-being. To achieve this heightened level of spiritual awareness takes time and commitment. If many of us spend most of our waking hours in the workplace—which is not, in most cases, associated with nurturing souls and spirits—can we continue to separate work and spirituality?

Countless numbers of employees have told me the implicit message they receive at work: "Leave your feelings at the door." Where did this hidden rule come from, and why does it have to be this way? We cannot be in touch with our spirituality if we are not in touch with our feelings. This "no-talk rule" naturally creates jammed emotional energy that stifles the growth of the spirit at work. To express care is considered "soft" in many companies and organizations, yet the "soft stuff," our emotional competence, drives most workplace decisions.

It is common knowledge that a few key leaders at the top shape a work environment. When I read some years ago that 38 percent of CEOs grew up in alcoholic families (four times the national average), it helped me understand what underlying issue is driving business. Shame. Yevgeny Yevtushenko, the Russian poet, said that "shame is the most powerful motivator of human progress."

While there has been enormous focus on "dysfunctional families," we seem to have ignored the fact that these same family members go to work! They, and we, bring our unfinished business into the workplace, creating negative, or toxic, energy that squelches creativity and productivity. Whether in the boardroom or the pulp mill, at the checkout line or the airline ticket counter, the issues are the same. The CEO, bookkeeper, electrician, and support person all face human issues at work.

We need some kind of spiritual Drano to release the combination of conscious and unconscious negative intentions and feelings—the intangibles—that drive the dynamics at work. Instead of spreading our discontent, we can choose to spread love and compassion. Fortunately, many business leaders are addressing spirituality in the workplace. While this indicates some progress, we continue to see that the majority of folks are still discouraged, cynical, suspicious, and mistrusting regarding their work culture.

Many of us spend our greatest number of waking hours at work; work matters. Work can give us a purpose, a sense of belonging, and can be a major source of self-esteem. Why wouldn't we choose to welcome spiritual growth in the workplace?

Regardless of whether our employers embrace spirituality, we can do it individually. Whatever light we shine will spread. The goodness we emanate is contagious. All we need to do is make the daily commitment. If we can remind ourselves to "be" at work a day at a time, perhaps we can keep our spirit ignited at work.

My own life has been greatly enriched by believing in the spirit in each of us. My hope is that the reflections in this book will inspire you to ignite your own spirit.

January

"The fresh start is always an illusion but a necessary one."

—Eleanor Clark

When was the last time you decided to make a change or to approach something differently? When we recognize the opportunity for a fresh start, we recognize our innate desire to change and grow. Although we often discover—perhaps as early as March—that we have forgotten our New Year's resolution, we may have gained three months of practicing who we want to be. These do count; they are in our history. They are cumulative. What's important is that we *do* make a commitment to change; we "give ourselves over," as *mittere*, the root of the word *commitment*, suggests.

Kathy had made a New Year's resolution—to share her honest opinions at staff meetings. She was fully committed to this new behavior. She asked two good friends at work to hold her accountable by observing her behavior. Kathy kept her word; soon the new behavior took hold. Others commented respectfully on what they saw. Kathy felt pleased with herself and gained self-esteem.

Just for today, I will resolve to keep my promises to myself. And although I may not do it perfectly, I will work toward my resolution for the new beginning.

January 2 ～ *Spiritual Flatness*

"Spirituality is like the flu; some get it—some don't."

—Huston Smith

Spiritual flatness is our nation's number one dis-ease. If we check our spirit at the door when we enter work and rely only on our left brain—our rational brain—we contribute to an environment of spiritual flatness. To bring our spirit to work means simply that we bring our whole selves to work, including our feelings and our current state of being.

We can begin by breathing consciously (the word *breath* comes from the root word *spiritus*); by doing so, we start to connect with our true selves. Being in touch with our spirit also means that we focus on our own center while recognizing we are not the center of anyone else's universe. We are drawn to spiritual vitality—an environment filled with the energy of "feeling" people. Yet even if we work in an environment that doesn't traditionally value the "spiritual" (medical, scientific, and so on) and instead focuses on efficiency, order, and intellect, we can maintain our focus on a personal level. We can always focus consciously on our breathing.

Just for today, I will be in touch with my feelings. I will focus on my breathing as often as I can throughout the workday.

"Silence isn't always golden, you know. Sometimes it's just plain yellow."

—Jan Kemp

When we are completely honest, our voices speak our values. Truth telling builds our integrity. Often we witness deception, injustice, and unfairness in the workplace—injustices that involve us personally or those we are responsible for. And often we walk away from encounters or meetings mumbling disparagingly to ourselves, "Why was I silent? Why did I just walk away?" One voice I carry inside of me is that of my mother who often said, "That will not do!" Such an internal voice is often countered by another: "Do you really think it's wise to speak out on *this one?*" Both voices live within all of us. We choose which voices we will hear and which advice we will act on. We consider the consequences; we consider the person we are addressing; and we take stands—where it matters.

In business seminars we hear stories of people who took high-risk stands on ethical matters. Repeatedly, these people describe how such acts deepened their character, helped them live with integrity, and allowed them to like who they saw in the mirror.

Just for today, I will be aware of what I give voice to and what I acknowledge in silence. I will trust myself in knowing where and to whom I shall speak the truth.

January 4 ~ Feelings

*"Why is it that people who cannot show feeling presume that
that is a strength and not a weakness? . . . People who cannot
feel punish those who do."*

—May Sarton

In my work, I often conduct confidential interviews to
learn about a company's work culture. I usually ask,
"What are the implicit rules, the unspoken rules, that
most people have to follow around here?" The typical
response is "Check your feelings at the door." Jack, a senior scientist, told of reading a poem aloud to honor his
co-worker Bob, who was retiring. Upon finishing the
poem, he looked up to staring faces and silence. No one
spoke; finally Bob thanked him. Jack felt punished for
breaking the no-feeling rule. This raised the question,
How can we be in touch with our spirit, our whole self,
if we cannot recognize our feelings eight hours a day?
Being in touch does not mean we have to talk about all
our feelings; it means being aware of feelings and how
they can drive our mood and behavior. If we are conscious and accepting of our own feelings, we naturally
extend the same acceptance to our co-workers.

*Just for today, I will be vulnerable enough to stay in touch with
and to honor my feelings.*

"We cannot not change."

—Paul Watzlawick

How comfortable it is when we can be in charge of our changes—when they are voluntary! Yet often change comes as a surprise, and this is when we are truly challenged. It may be a job transfer, a promotion, a new boss—or a layoff. Some people fare well in rocky boats and enjoy the chaos of uncertainty; others fear the unknown. If we can accept that every molecule in the human body replaces itself every seven years, why do we have such difficulty recognizing that some beliefs and ways might also need to change every seven years? Our old photo albums reveal how quickly our physical bodies change. Mental changes come more slowly and may be more difficult to identify. Recall some of your "I used to thinks."

Resisting change does not bode well in a world that is constantly changing. We must ask ourselves what we really fear with change and use change as an opportunity for growth.

Just for today, I will acknowledge that I will continue to change. I can choose to let go.

January 6 ⁓ Guilt and Values

"Guilt is not a cul de sac; there is always a way out. Guilt says 'I made a mistake'; shame says 'I am a mistake.'"

—Merle A. Fossum and Marilyn Mason

Guilt differs from shame. While shame is about "who I am," guilt is about "what I do." Whenever we violate our values and our core beliefs, we feel guilt. Conversely, we can use guilt as a cue that we have violated one of our values. For example, if I value my responsibility to others, I will be accountable to others and feel guilt if I do not follow through. When we know that we have been part of a problem at work, we can acknowledge that and can say, "I'm wrong, I'm sorry. I made a mistake." By owning our behavior, we can keep the connection alive in the relationship.

Often "healthy guilting" is a useful tool in the workplace. When we allow subordinates or co-workers a "way out" by changing their behavior or by completing the unfinished task, we are offering them an opportunity to take responsibility for their behaviors and thus claim their values. By offering a way back from the guilt, their self-esteem can be intact.

Just for today, I will accept my healthy guilt and know it is a pathway to know better what my values are and make the necessary changes to live them.

Competition ⌒ January 7

"To be my best I need you . . . swimming beside me."

—Mariah Burton-Nelson

How often do we find ourselves comparing our work or our success with someone else? While facing our competitive edge can be healthy and stimulating, just what does it do when those people are peers in the office? Competition, like anything else, can be carried to extremes. Susan realized that she felt competitive with Amy; even though they were in different divisions, she often felt suspicious. This dynamic kept Susan on her toes and highly motivated. One day Susan heard herself making a slightly dishonest statement about Amy when an outside client commented on Amy's competence. Susan immediately felt sick; she had gone too far.

Competition *can* give us that edge to keep ahead—to push a little harder—toward our own improvement. When our push comes from within, we compete with our own previous record. Many of us respond to someone "swimming" beside us. We recognize that it is that "other" who can let us know we all contribute. The question is, can we look next to us, as well as within?

Just for today, I will compete with myself, recognizing that others are "swimming" in the lanes next to me, and that if I am doing the best I can, we can all succeed.

"Ambition, if it [is] to be savored, let alone achieved, [has] to be rooted in possibility."

—P. D. James

Many of us grew up with the message that it is not all right to be overtly ambitious. Many of us have often strived unconsciously, setting goals and reaching for that next rung, yet at the same time never thinking we were ambitious. I recall my first rock-climbing trip, during which I stood very frightened at the edge of a cliff over the water. The leaders had trained us in rock-craft skills; I was physically secure. Yet, suddenly I felt tears streaming down my face. After asking myself what my fears were about (was it height, trust, falling?), I sputtered, "I'm afraid I won't achieve." I was dumbfounded at this discovery. While our culture gives men permission to be ambitious, it trains women to deny their ambitions. Perhaps this lies in *Merriam-Webster's Collegiate Dictionary's* definition of *ambition:* "an ardent desire for rank, fame, or power." Yet, *Webster's* also defines *ambition* as a "desire to achieve a particular end." I think the latter is the definition that can motivate both men and women.

Just for today, I shall stay focused on the big picture of where I am going, knowing I can climb toward my goal, a step at a time.

Stress ~ January 9

"The bow always strung . . . will not do."

—George Eliot

How do you cope with stress? Our lives are filled with stress—sometimes it's work related; sometimes it comes from home. Stress is not an event in itself; rather, it is how we respond to given events. For some of us, stress is alive and palpable; for others it sneaks into our bodies and finds a harbor in one of our organs, leading to physical illness. Most people know the top major life stressors—job changes, moves, deaths and losses, divorce. Yet we often forget that positive events are also stressful. Recently, when leaving my new home where I felt pleased and excited, I suddenly became anxious and confused. I could not find my handbag or my shoes, and I needed to get to the airport. I stood still and began to breathe deeply. I talked out loud about what I had to do and in what order. I pictured an imaginary cup to store my stress. Suddenly, I found my bag and my shoes!

Just for today, I will ask myself how I cope with stress. I will imagine a cup to hold my stress, take a deep breath, and move forward one step at a time.

January 10 ~ *Learning*

"The excitement of learning separates youth from old age. As long as you're learning you're not old."

—Rosalyn S. Yalow

I believe that if you are not learning, you are not living. What is more exciting than learning? A group of managers in a technology firm were totally unaware about how they came across to people. They trod on other people's feelings, gave very little feedback, and furthermore, thought that employees should not need recognition or appreciation ("their salaries tell them that"). When three key people left the company within a short period, they decided to call for help. The group's feeling-expressiveness level was at the lowest level of emotional maturity. We had to start where the group was and not judge. I asked them if they were willing to be learners. We began with personal check-ins in the meetings in which they could describe their feelings with the four basic, "mad," "sad," "glad," or "scared" or anything within that range. Soon they learned how they came across to one another and got feedback from one another. They became quite excited about their learning and discoveries and were eager to create changes in their workplace.

Just for today, I can be a learner. I do not need to know all the answers. And as I can learn more about me, I can learn more about my co-workers.

"Attitude is everything."

Have you ever had to work with someone who had a negative attitude—a person who whines and is cynical of management? Our attitudes affect our productivity; a negative attitude can slow down our work. If we could measure the negative energy charge in the air, we could learn much about the productivity level of any given workplace. While healthy skepticism—through asking questions and seeking higher standards of performance—can add vitality to the workplace, a negative or cynical attitude is like putting toxins in the air. We feel it. Usually those who hide from possibilities in their negative attitudes are fearful—fearful that they might be truly hurt or disappointed again. They had risked before with positive attitudes and had felt betrayed. Negative attitudes not only affect our work environment, they also affect our overall health. A positive attitude can be inspiring to those around us and create an environment in which people can be productive. Most of all, it can contribute to our sense of well-being throughout the day.

Just for today, I will focus on finding the positives, however small. It is up to me; my attitude will determine what my day can be.

January 12 ~ *Communication*

"We cannot not *communicate."*

—Paul Watzlawick

So often we hear the words *We don't communicate!* But of course we do; we communicate through our facial expressions, our silences, our body language. This type of nonverbal communication is five times more believable than our words, often revealing our most honest message. Most of our nonverbal communication is unconscious. And when our self-awareness is low, we may be totally out of touch with the messages we convey. When we "read" the communication of others, we often find it hard to find people credible if they are saying something sincerely in words but looking away or over our shoulder while speaking. Or, if someone tries to tell us how relaxed he or she is but we see this person incessantly kicking a leg, we find his or her words hard to believe. Sometimes we feel misunderstood. What is important to recognize is that the meaning is made by the listener. It is not what we say that makes the difference; it is what the listener hears. For this reason, we need to choose our words and our behavior carefully, especially when we're trying to convey an important message.

Just for today, I will focus on communicating clear, congruent messages. I will be mindful of my nonverbal communication.

"All self-knowledge is purchased at the cost of guilt."

—Paul Tillich

What do you feel guilty about? We all experience feelings of guilt—for example, when we are late or fail to attend an event after we have given someone our word. Yet guilt can be a positive force in our lives. We can use feelings of guilt to identify what our true values are; we feel guilt when we violate something that is important to us. Guilt—which is a feeling we have about a particular behavior, unlike shame, which is a feeling we have about who we are—offers the opportunity to correct the action that violated our ethics. Guilt signals that we have to make some amends; we can repair the "broken bridge" in the relationship. It's often helpful to think about two kinds of guilt—healthy guilt and neurotic guilt. If we break our word with someone, we feel healthy guilt. Such guilt tells us we owe an apology. On the other hand, if we feel guilty every time we have to say no to anyone, we are entering into neurotic guilt. This is guilt that stems from old and faded beliefs that come from someone else's voices, not our own.

Just for today, I will take charge of my guilt and recognize which is growth-serving healthy guilt and which is the "rope worn thin" neurotic guilt that comes from childhood voices.

January 14 ⌒ *Overresponsibility*

"Only lies and evil come from letting people off."

—Iris Murdoch

John struggled. He did not know how to handle a work situation that was deeply affecting his entire work group. His subordinate Mark was not treating people with respect and was secretive when challenged. In addition, he was taking credit for other people's work. One of John's assistants asked him why he was giving so much power to Mark and not confronting his inappropriate behavior. John quickly replied, "I don't want to lay him flat out." His colleague reminded John that he was not responsible *for* Mark; he was responsible *to* Mark and to the company's core values. Indeed, it was John's responsibility to give constructive feedback to Mark and help him grow professionally. John had created a lose-lose situation. In "protecting" Mark, he had violated his own integrity. John began to see how his overprotection was sabotaging the entire work group. John went to Mark and acted responsibly—he cited the behaviors that needed changing, held him accountable for changes to be made, and set up weekly meetings for progress reports.

Just for today, I will be responsible to my peers and subordinates. I will be responsible for my own thoughts and feelings and recognize that I am not responsible for the feelings of others.

"As you change, so does the system around you."

—Rene Schwartz

Most companies recognize that the work environment greatly influences profits, safety, and employee retention. Today many companies see the value of using the workplace as a setting for personal growth and change. For years it was believed that the home was where people developed skills; we have found that this is simply not true for all. Thus, three major life skills now being taught at work are cooperation, fair fighting, and respect for differences. We refer to these ideas as "team building," "conflict resolution," and "cultural diversity." Often, because the workplace has substantial control over people's lives, they seem to learn readily there. Companies large and small are creating work systems where human skill development is normalized. Small firms as well as large are recognizing the importance of helping people change and grow. When we learn these skills at work, we can also take them home and bridge the gap between who we are at work and who we are at home. Both our work system and our family system can change.

Just for today, I will be open to growing at work and recognize that as I change, so does the system around me.

January 16 ⌒ *Leadership*

"No leader can be too far ahead of his [or her] followers."

—Eleanor Roosevelt

Whom do you lead, and how? We all have experiences in leading others—perhaps at work, in community, or in our family lives. It could be in a small work group, your family, your community, or through a role in the church, temple, or mosque. What do you know about your leadership style? Can you identify the traits that make you a good leader? Think of leaders you respect; we often discover that people with important titles are not necessarily effective leaders. In conducting leadership seminars, I have learned that a wide range of traits are attributed to leaders. Today we hear much about "authentic" leadership. Yet we must realize that many authentic leaders are not people of high integrity. Many of our true leaders are not famous yet have led well through the years. These people are visionaries; they're innovative, collaborative, supportive of others, and respond well to criticism. How would you rate yourself on the above qualities? To lead others, we must become aware of our leadership style and how we motivate others so they want to follow.

Just for today, I will pay attention to how I lead. I will ask myself what I have to offer in leadership traits. I will ask myself what areas need development.

"Humor is a rubber sword—it allows you to make a point without drawing blood."

—Mary Hirsch

Humor at work is a sign of a vital work system. Laughing is good for our brains; when we laugh, endorphins are released and contribute to a state of well-being. We all know that humor is a great stress reducer; laughter is "internal jogging." It takes much less energy to smile than to frown, and it causes fewer wrinkles. However, laughing at the expense of others is not humor; rather, it is sarcasm or mild cruelty.

Can you laugh at yourself? If we are going to keep our spirits awake at work, we need to be able to tell funny stories about ourselves. Humor helps us connect with others. A friend of mine was presenting a diversity workshop in her office. She was very aware of the sensitive gender issues at the company. She chose to use humor to deliver her important messages. Always teasingly referred to as the company's "gender cop," she communicated all the points she wanted to make, with humor. She felt heard, and everyone praised her words.

Just for today, I will use the antidote of humor to relieve my stress. I will focus on not taking life too seriously.

January 18 ~ *Gossip*

"Gossip is the opiate of the oppressed."

—Erica Jong

Some people talk about ideas; some people talk about people. With which group would you identify? Have you ever felt "special" because someone shared a piece of gossip with you? You probably recognized that you were joining in a game that did not feel good. When we gossip, we might ask what is going on in our own lives that we need to try to elevate ourselves momentarily (and falsely) to feel a bit above someone else. Have you ever learned that someone said something mean or untrue about you? It hurts, doesn't it? When we gossip, we are also saying something about ourselves.

Gossip creates an unsafe work environment; people become suspicious and are fearful to be known. One company developed a unique pattern. If someone came to Patty with some gossip about Jane, for example, Patty would say, "Come, let's go over to Jane so you can say that directly to her." In that particular company, new norms were established. People learned that gossip would not be tolerated.

Just for today, I will not gossip. If someone engages me in gossip, I will make a "graceful exit" and be true to my higher self who does not need to judge others.

"I know the lights are on, but there's nobody home inside."

—Author unknown

When was the last time you were talking with someone and felt that the other person "left you"? A departure is very clear when people visibly walk away from us, but it is another thing when people "leave" psychologically. Dr. Pauline Boss of the University of Minnesota, a family stress researcher, studied the wartime Missing in Action (MIA) families during and after the Vietnam War and found that the surviving families kept the MIAs alive by setting their place at the table or by keeping their rooms intact, as though they were still alive. The family member was gone physically but kept alive psychologically. After learning about Boss's studies, I realized that it seemed that I worked with the opposite: addicted or compulsive people were physically present but often psychologically absent.

At times we all become overly stressed or otherwise preoccupied; when this happens, we do often "leave" others, unaware that we are abandoning them. To minimize the harm that this "leaving" can inflict—some people assume they were not interesting because someone left them psychologically—we need to recognize our stress level and be honest about what we are going through. This shows respect for others and helps them understand our absences.

Just for today, I will pay full attention when speaking with others. If I am too stressed to listen, I will acknowledge that I cannot be fully present and will ask to talk at another time.

January 20 ~ *Boundaries*

"A boundary between self and not-self is the first one we draw and the last one we erase."

—Ken Wilbur

Much is written about boundaries. We can see how well we manage boundaries by looking at how we manage the line of respect between ourselves and others. I recall one initial interview with a coaching candidate. He strode across my office, brushing lightly the handshake I offered, and walked directly to the corner where there was a long table. He sat on top of the table, picked up my telephone, and called someone. I stood at the door nonplussed! Nowhere in my professional training had I been trained to deal with such rudeness; they didn't teach "boundary management" in my training or course work. I wondered how this man's boundaries had been violated—and later learned about the physical abuse in his childhood.

The question is, How do I manage my own boundaries? How often do we interrupt conversations, or sneak into a line, or invade another's personal space? We know how we feel when others enter our personal space without our permission; are we aware of how we intrude into other people's space?

Just for today, I will be mindful of my boundaries—trusting my inner sense of where my comfort level is—and of my own behavior as it affects other people's boundaries.

"The role of the leader is to create the future, not manage the past."

—Adrian Levy

People who actively create their futures embrace a vision and believe in it. Do you have a vision, a personal vision, for yourself? Do you know your company's vision? Where do you want to be in ten years? Scott Adams, the cartoonist who created the popular "Dilbert" comic strip, said that he had a vision; he decided to become one of the top cartoonists in America. Indeed, he has done that. Artist Carole LaRoche recounts that when she left Boston as a housewife and moved to Santa Fe, New Mexico, she decided to declare herself an artist. Yes, Carole had had art training some years ago before her homemaking/parenting years, but when she came to Santa Fe, she decided that she was going to be an artist. She did just that and her work is now internationally known. A billboard advertising a metropolitan community college states, "If You Don't Follow Your Dream, Who Will?" When we commit to a vision, we take the steps to create the future we seek.

Just for today, I will look ahead and carry a vision in my mind for the future I can create.

January 22 ~ *Believing in Yourself*

"Once we believe in ourselves we can risk curiosity, wonder, spontaneous delight or any experience that reveals the human spirit."

—e. e. cummings

Once, when nominated for presidency of a national professional organization, I commented to a friend that I did not know whether I could vote for myself. It felt awkward. My friend replied, "Well, if you won't vote for you, why should anyone else?" I got the message and realized what she was talking about: it was knowing that I had to believe in myself in order to vote for me—or to ask others to vote for me. When we believe in and stand up for ourselves, we are teaching others how to treat us. When our belief in ourselves is low, we give our power to other people to tell us who we are, what opinions to hold, and how to act. When we believe in ourselves, we allow others to know who we are. We do not overinvest in pleasing or accommodating others. When we believe in ourselves, we do not need to "honk our own horns." Rather, we can carry that knowing quietly within us; it will be reflected outward.

Just for today, I will say to myself, "I believe in me and what I stand for, and I will communicate that to others."

". . . the immediate shudder which runs through me from head to foot without any discursive preparation . . . the internal hemorrhage."

—Jean-Paul Sartre

How does shame affect who you are at work? Do you shame others? Do others shame you? Shame is that invisible dragon that creates the "internal hemorrhage" that flows through us; our self feels diminished and we feel unworthy as human beings. Shame is the "self judging the self"—self-put-downs and self-criticism abound. We avoid shame; we get blaming, angry, helpless, or depressed in response to a shaming interaction. Years ago my family visited Universal Studios and saw how the murder scene in the film *Psycho* was created. Hollywood blood was Hershey's Chocolate Syrup, contained in capsules wired onto the actor's body. When the off-stage person tapped the keys on the typewriter-like machine, the chocolate "hemorrhage" began on the actor's body. Shame is similar; someone (off our stage) says something to us or even gives a certain look or question. Our shame is tapped. Often we work in shame-bound systems in which we can experience shame and cut ourselves off. The shame becomes a downward spiral; it has a cul-de-sac.

Just for today, I will pay attention to where I see shame in my workplace and let myself know when I shame others or feel shamed by others.

January 24 〜 Envy

"Some folks are always thirsting for water from other people's wells."

—Jessamyn West

Envy strikes when we feel resentful or painfully aware of another's advantage. How does envy affect your work life? How do you handle your feelings when someone else is awarded a coveted promotion or achieves some outstanding success? How do you handle it when you know that you do not want to be that person, but still would like to know what that experience might be like? Do you allow yourself to have a fleeting moment of envy, or do you deepen it into resentment and deep jealousy? Or a grudge? It has been said that spite is never lonely; envy always tags along. Envy can eat away at our insides; perhaps that is the source of the phrase "green with envy." Every time we spend our energy envying what others have, we walk away from our own true paths. We need to stay true to ourselves and to what we need to do to shape our own destinations. When we focus on the accomplishments of others, we walk away from our self and our goals.

Just for today, I will acknowledge that I can be human enough to be touched by envy, but I will celebrate my own accomplishments and honor my true path. I will send good wishes to those I am envious of.

"Assumptions are the doorway to judgments."

—Anonymous

When was the last time you discovered that you had misjudged a situation because of an assumption you made? Often we assume because we simply do not understand, and perhaps choose not to. Our assumptions can rapidly lead to judgments. When we do not verify information and assume that we know the truth, we feed into our own beliefs. Our assumptions can block our capacity to hear one another. Not long ago in a management meeting, I asked the group to list what assumptions they might have to put aside to truly hear one another. The leader of the group said that each time he was aware of "assuming" something, he would hold his ear. It was fascinating to see the others join in and how frequently the ears were tugged during our meeting. What if we could always be that conscious of the assumptions we make about a colleague, a boss, or a subordinate? With such self-knowledge, we just might seek the truth—and end up getting to know and liking a co-worker.

Just for today, I will ask myself what I might be assuming about others. I will ask myself, "How do I know?"

January 26 ~ *Time as Respect*

"If we take care of the moments, the years will take care of themselves."

—Maria Edgeworth

When visiting a colleague at her home for the first time, I arrived late. After I gave an apologetic greeting, she stood with her feet planted firmly, looked me in the eye, and asked, "Mason, I want to know one thing—who the hell do you think you are that you can show up so late and still have as many friends as you do?" That moment was life changing. Her directness about my lack of consideration for others had only one meaning for me—disrespect. I had never thought of myself as disrespectful toward my friends and colleagues; I used the term "Irish time" for arriving late. Yet I lived in America, not Ireland. I later thanked her for the gift she gave me. I don't know when in my adult life I changed a perception and behavior so immediately. My friends, who had long accommodated the lateness, were pleased to learn I now kept my word. Promptness is a sign of respect and good boundaries.

Just for today, I shall focus on managing my time well enough to treat all people with the same measure of respect.

"Alas, we give our own coloring to the actions of others."

—L. E. Landon

Recently, when working with a sarcastic and critical management group, I did not feel safe. After sending out a meeting agenda via e-mail, the return e-mail from the chair said, "Simply cannot understand this garbled junk. Please resend." I was stunned. This could not be true of the sender; he was stable, solid, and respectful. "Now they're including me in the mean-spiritedness," I told myself. I decided to wait a few days before responding. I surely did not want to put him down; nor was I willing to accept being talked to in this way. In a few days I responded in an inquiring manner about the "garbled junk." The response was immediate: "When I referred to the garbled junk, I was not referring to your report; all that came through on the attachment was a page filled with small squares and computer symbols—in other words, 'garbled junk.'" What a lesson! How easy it is to make judgments about others—when we really do not have all the pieces to the puzzle.

Just for today, I will be sure to check out thoroughly my judgmental interpretations. I shall receive messages with a fresh, responsive, and open attitude.

January 28 ⌒ *Perfectionism*

"Perfectionism is the voice of the oppressor."

—Anne Lamott

Emily knew she was a perfectionist. It had served her well. She was a dedicated manager, always striving to do her best and willing to put in extra time to accomplish her goals. So focused on her work, she did not realize how her perfectionism affected those around her. Her high standards spilled over to her subordinates. Her children always felt "lesser than" in her presence. After Emily spent years managing her group with controlling perfectionism, the president called her into his office to discuss her behavior. He told her that employees in her division lasted only half as long as in the other regional managers' teams and directed her to begin delegating and stop micromanaging. Emily felt devastated. She was distraught; she thought her entire world was coming apart. Perfectionism often is born out of shame; it is for many the need to avoid criticism and to build self-esteem. Yet, when we allow ourselves to make mistakes, when we're gentle with ourselves, we're able to forgive ourselves.

Just for today, I will allow myself to be human—I do not have to be perfect. If perfectionism surfaces, I will ask myself what shame is driving me.

*"When you know you have to swallow a toad, don't look at it
too long."*

—Anonymous

Have you ever wanted to lie about something? I recall when I was behind in turning over some of these pages to my editor. Some personal family issues had taken me from my writing, but that did not seem like a sufficient excuse. I could have called my editor earlier to explain the situation. Now I faced the deadline and realized I would not make it. I had to make that telephone call; I thought about it daily. Yet the truth seemed flimsy, not good enough. I wanted to lie; I even rehearsed some lines. Then my computer crashed and I thought, "Now that's a legitimate out." But it restored almost immediately. Finally, I decided that the best path was the only path—the truth. Face the consequences. In the end, the agony of waiting and delaying was much more difficult than telling the truth.

Just for today, I will tell the truth. I will take responsibility for my actions and face the consequences.

January 30 ～ *Personal Power*

"Genuine power is power-with—pseudo power is power-over."

—M. P. Follett

What M. P. Follett describes here is a good example of what personal power is about. Many people can achieve role power; that is, power through a title or wealth or fame. But that never equals personal power. Personal power is reflected through our grown-upness. Personal power refers to our own sense of who we are and includes our sense of self-worth. How do we read personal power in other people? We can read personal power by observing how others enter a room; they need not speak. Often in leadership seminars I ask participants to "walk the rug." Flanked on either side by other participants, the person walking is asked to simply walk down the middle of the floor or rug. The group members then use a single word or short phrases to provide feedback on what they saw. Some may hear "confidence," "timidity," "caution," and so on. All these words give the "walker" a sense of his or her personal power. It is a reminder that our personal power is observable by others; our self-respect shines through to others.

Just for today, I will tune in to myself, stay with myself, and recognize that my nonverbal behavior does not lie. I will be the truest me I can be . . . just for this day.

"Secrecy is as indispensable to human beings as fire, and as greatly feared."

—Sissela Bok

Have you ever walked into a work setting and just sensed the presence of secrets? Secrets carry their own life energy; we can almost feel a secret in the group—it fills the room. What we need to recognize at these moments is that the secrets may be necessary. For example, perhaps this is a management secret that cannot be shared at this time. When George received word that his plant would be closing just before Christmas, he knew he could not release the news until the company had made it public. Carrying the secret became a burden for George, but he knew he needed to keep this confidence. He was concerned that, if leaked, his secret could create suspicion and mistrust. The line between privacy and secrecy in the workplace is a fine one. On the other hand, some secrets serve no purpose and are only destructive. These secrets, often gossip, tend to create a toxic environment, one in which it is hard to trust or feel safe. Often secrets can hold power.

Just for today, if I sense secrecy, I will trust that knowing. I shall ask myself if perhaps I am sensing that there is a change in the air that cannot be shared. Or, am I truly sensing that toxic gossipy secrets are jamming the energy at work?

February

"Codependency refers to the behavior that accommodates the needs of others to the neglect of one's self."

In the late 1980s, in the heat of the codependency movement in America (the fastest-growing social movement of the twentieth century), a seminar participant offered a company speaker a glass of water. Her colleague snidely commented, "Well, aren't you being the codependent one, though!" Stunned, the woman replied, "Why no, not at all; I'm simply being considerate." Her colleague had carried the definition of codependency to an extreme, thinking that any helping act was dysfunctional behavior. When we behave "codependently," we are attempting to avoid taking responsibility for our own lives and well-being. By focusing on others, we attempt to control others by putting their needs first. This kind of "help" hinders the growth of everyone involved. Naturally, there are times when extreme care is necessary. When John returned to work after the death of his eleven-year-old child, his team came forth to help carry the workload. Codependent behavior does *not* refer to kindness and considerate actions; rather, it is caring taken to an extreme to the detriment of oneself.

Just for today, I will ask myself to recognize the difference between my acts of caring and my need to be controlling.

February 2 ⌢ *Values*

"These [values] are the basic concepts and beliefs of an organization; as such they form the heart of the corporate culture."

—Terrence Deal and Allan Kennedy

Most of us think of our values as high ideals of worth—our ethics—yet how often do we find ourselves not "walking our talk"? It helps to distinguish a *belief* from a *value*. A belief is something we consider to be true—a principle we hold. When we act on that belief, we are then making it a value. Many define value as a belief plus action. For example, if we value promptness as a sign of respect, we show up on time. We can also use our feelings to identify our values conflicts at work. When we feel an internal charge—some reactivity—to a direction at work, we often feel anger or tension. If we turn that strong feeling over, we can often discover what value is under our response. Values conflicts—especially when we see greed and ruthless ambition in another—can serve as a reminder to hold to our own values.

Just for today, I will honor my values. I will rate my five most important values and ask myself whether I'm walking my talk, or at least walking toward my talk.

"We are most deeply asleep at the switch when we fancy we control any switches at all."

—Annie Dillard

A colleague once said, "When I was a schoolboy, I recall that when some kids took intramural sports and some took band, I took control!" For many of us, our need to control was born out of early childhood experiences in which we felt powerless and insecure. Grabbing on to some little corner of life gave us something to call our own. We may have needed that then. In our adult lives, however, we often needlessly carry those old patterns. Control, when focused on our own work efforts, is a positive force. We need control to have order in life. To be "controlling" is another matter. Fed by domination, helplessness, insecurity, or intimidation, control produces competition, overresponsibility, shame, and mistrust. When we're in control of our own behavior, we can better distinguish between being in control of others and being controlling. Controlling behavior can give the illusion of power over others—for the moment. Yet deep inside we know that we ultimately have to surrender that control and recognize the delusions in our controlling behaviors.

Just for today, I will trust that the only person I can be in real control of is myself. I will ask myself what I fear losing if I am not in control. Today, I will ask my Higher Power to help me learn the difference between control *and* controlling.

February 4 〜 *Failure*

"Perhaps it is not failure at all; it is simply feedback."

—Virginia Satir

How do you know when a failure is a failure? Is failure the discovery that you have not met your goals? While it's natural to feel failure when we have not succeeded in a new role or new project, there is also another side to failure. Perhaps it is simply feedback that you are on the wrong path. Some people avoid facing failure by not taking risks. Yet if we are going to have successes, we must take risks. Some ventures will have positive outcomes; other outcomes will inform us that the time is not right or there is another direction. This is feedback, pure and simple. When we accept that our choices are going to tell us something positive or negative, we must be ready to accept and learn from the outcomes. If we are unable to face failures, or feedback, when we take the different turn, we will become stuck. We will avoid risking; we will become controlling and rigid. This is a high price to pay for a misinterpretation of the word *failure*.

Just for today, I will not view outcomes as failures. I shall know that I will never have 100 percent return on choices I make. I will strive to examine outcomes as feedback to lead me where I need to go.

Cynicism ～ February 5

"A cynical person is almost the saddest sight to see, because it means that he or she has gone from knowing nothing to believing in nothing."

—Maya Angelou

Merriam-Webster's Collegiate Dictionary defines *cynical* as being "contemptuously distrustful of human nature and motives." Have you ever noticed how the cynics appear when a company attempts to introduce a new program or approach to business? The "ain't it awful" club is often an informal structure within organizations. It surely allows people to unite through blame and doubt. Cynicism, if too prevalent, can keep the system stuck. How do you feel after you have joined the circle of cynics? These are the people who will always think in the "us-them" mode. They will look for what has not happened. Some voice their opinions with righteous indignation. Cynics often base their opinions on judgments, on little data. I wonder if cynicism is not connected to fear—fear of real change, fear about one's own capabilities, or the fear of risking advancement. If we belong to the circle of cynicism, we can always comment on change as "the program of the week" and thus contribute to sabotaging the process of any real and lasting change.

Just for today, I shall be aware of the slide into cynicism and shall politely distance myself from those who wish to live in toxic energy.

February 6 ～ Purpose

"Nothing contributes so much to tranquilize the mind as a steady purpose—a point on which the soul may fix its intellectual eye."

—Mary Shelley

Do you know what your purpose is in life? Writer and speaker Malidoma Somé describes purpose when he talks about his small home village in Africa, Birkina Fasso. When a child is born, the villagers gather 'round to name the child. The child's name will stand for the purpose to be fulfilled by that child's presence. Many of us do not consider what our purpose is in this world until we enter late adulthood. Yet knowing our purpose in being where we are in our workplace can help us keep our sails set. It takes many roles within an organization to fulfill the company's mission. Where would Wal-Mart or Target or the Bell systems be without their hardworking employees who strive to serve us well? One remarkable example is Whole Foods, the organic food chain, whose employees think and live "team." It does not matter what status level one has within the organization; all the team members are there to serve. They seem to know what their purpose is and they work with a shared purpose.

Just for today, I will honor my purpose. If I have not done so yet, I shall start a rough draft of what my purpose in life is. This is the life I bring to my work.

"We don't get offered crises; they arrive."

—Elizabeth Janeway

How do you handle your personal crises when you are at work? How do you hang on when your mind is filled with outside matters—matters of the heart? Our personal life crises—a sick child, a family member's surgery or chronic illness, or a troubled relationship with a loved one—can cause us to be less effective at work. Our minds drift; we may be rushing to the telephone to handle details or check on people. We are not fully present. When we are living with crisis, it is important to let someone know. This does not mean telling "all," but it helps when you can let your boss or co-worker know you cannot be fully present. When Jack was acting distant and unwilling to participate in his group's meetings, the group leader finally asked what was going on; he thought Jack no longer cared about his work. When Jack revealed that he was going through a child custody hearing in his divorce, the group became understanding and supportive.

Just for today, I shall accept that my personal crisis can affect my work. Tomorrow is another day!

February 8 ⁓ *Being Present*

"Wherever you go, there you are."

—Jon Kabat-Zinn

What does it mean to be fully present? How do we bring our whole self to the scene? Have you ever worked with someone who didn't seem to be quite "there"? Often we feel deserted when someone is standing in an empty shell with his or her mind elsewhere. Being fully present means that we can really hear others; we can enter into true dialogue; we can read situations well. Being fully present means that we can access our intuition and feel our connections to others. Our colleagues and friends will feel heard. Being fully present means being as aware as we can be; it means looking people in the eye when we speak with them. It means we allow ourselves to be still in the presence of chaos and busy-ness. Being present allows us to recognize the importance of tuning in to our true selves; it does not take any more time. In fact, it will actually save time because we will be able to retain the experience we are engaged in.

Just for today, let me be fully present with everyone with whom I am in contact.

"He's been living rent-free in my head too long."

—A seminar participant

Have you ever worked with someone who can "pull your chain" and you don't seem to know why? When we react strongly to someone else's behavior, we are giving that person the power to determine our feelings; we are no longer in charge of ourselves. We might even carry the reactive energy home with us and lose sleep over it. Often we use righteous indignation or false superiority as a defense to cover our feelings of powerlessness to impact or control another. The cost of reactivity can be high—sleepless nights, headaches, wasted hours of complaining (aloud or in silence)—not to mention the nonproductive work hours. We can burden friends and family members with our reactions. Helpful at first, this can quickly convert into wasted time and energy. In order to move beyond reactivity, we can ask, "Why am I giving this person so much power to affect me? Where have I known this before in my life—whom does this person remind me of?"

Just for today, I will examine my reactivity to learn more about me. Only I can take charge of my reactive responses. I know I cannot control others; I can only be in charge of me.

February 10 ❧ Teams

"Teamwork is the ability to work together toward a common vision. . . . It is the fuel that allows common people to attain uncommon results."

—*Harvard Business Review*

Is team building a part of your workplace? Being a member of a team provides many opportunities for personal growth. When we move from a large group into a team focus, we can learn about growing trust in relationships by being honest with one another. Teams are a place where we can explore our ideas. Perhaps most worthwhile is the experience of arriving at team decisions or developing plans, and recognizing the loneliness of making decisions as a single leader. Additionally, in a highly functioning team, conflict is embraced, and strategies for conflict are discussed openly. Of course, teams also teach us tolerance and patience.

Teams can be either formal or informal. Do you believe that you are a part of a group or a team in your workplace? How successful has your company been in encouraging teamwork? When companies truly form a "we" at work, creative problem solving and effective conflict resolution abound.

Just for today, I will examine where my "team" is at work, and if I don't have a formal team, I will begin to think "team" and reach out to create that spirit of "we" at work.

"She is a friend of my mind. She gather me, man. The pieces I am, she gather them and give them back to me in all the right order."

—Toni Morrison

Who are your friends at work? Are there people in your company whom you can count on and talk with when you need support? During Susan's first pregnancy, her women friends at the office gathered around her, offering their suggestions, their stories, and their sincere interest. Years ago people thought it was not good to have friends at work; the fear was that productivity would decrease. Indeed, a recent Gallup Poll showed that productivity increases according to the degree to which friendships are established at work. Susan was able to get support about morning sickness and could then get on with her work, feeling the supportive environment. Most of us are not surprised to learn that safety increases in the workplace when people consider their co-workers to be friends. If we are going to invest the high number of hours that we do at work, doesn't it make sense that we can feel good about going to spend the day with some friends?

Just for today, I will look around me and recognize who my friends are and who can help nourish my spirit at work.

February 12 ∽ *Family Matters*

"The first organization we belong to is our family."

Author unknown

Often we forget that we bring the "family inside us" to work. When Steve and Ellie were struggling to manage their division together, they did not realize that their family histories were involved. Growing up, Ellie's older brother had treated her badly. She had not realized that her childhood perceptions were the birthplace of her "process"—how she learned to be in the world, to see herself, and to be in relationships. These childhood perceptions shaped Ellie's interpretations of Steve's behavior. Such impaired perceptions also block our spiritual growth. After reading some material about family loyalties, Ellie decided not to stay within the confines of her childhood memories. She was excited to learn that she could choose not to be a reactor to the forces from her past.

At some point in our lives, we all have to betray our childhood loyalty to our families and create an adult loyalty. Once Ellie recognized that Steve was not her brother, they became a strong leadership pair.

Just for today, I will ask myself whether I hold on to any childhood beliefs that might affect my daily work relationships. If necessary, I will take that journey home.

"The ego always attempts to buy out the spirit."

—Anonymous

Our egos can be seduced at work—by titles, pay increases, or by feeling "favorite" to a superior at work. The ego is cunning; it can sneak into our psyches with lies, telling us that we are really very important, that no one can do this job but us, or that we really can have self-worth through a title. Our spirits need room to breathe at work; spirit connects with the right hemisphere of the brain—home of our unconscious, our nonverbal behavior. Our spirits speak to us through the language of feelings, of intuition. Our egos are important to us; they are the center of our conscious lives. When they're healthy, our egos are the strong, grounded, activating principle by which we make intellectual assessments and judgments, show feelings appropriately, and relate skillfully to others. In an unhealthy state, the ego becomes attached to outcomes, addicted, judgmental, and starts to panic, control, and dramatize life. Our goal is to keep a loving balance between the spirit and ego.

Just for today, I will focus on taking hold and letting go at the same time, recognizing that with this balance, my ego cannot buy out my spirit.

February 14 ⁓ *The Heart*

"What we have most to fear is failure of the heart."

—Sonia Johnson

How do you experience the heart at work? With whom? How is caring shown? Surely we do not need to hear expressions of deep feeling at work; we can simply tune into the acts and the energy that pervade our workplaces. When a business consultant asked a group, "How do you know you matter around here?" he was fascinated to hear the wide range of responses. Some people fell silent, others paused, and still others seemed confident in knowing they matter. Unfortunately, the latter group was small in number. In some company cultures, employees let one another know that they care. It may be shown in time off for an illness at home or a surprise informal celebration during the workday. The caring at work cannot be insincere; rituals that do not come from the heart are not trusted by employees. With support from the top, workers are typically not fearful to show their caring. The heart of an organization can be almost palpable when you enter the workplace.

Just for today, I will tune in to my own heart and be genuinely caring wherever possible.

"Your spirituality encompasses your whole soul's journey."

—Gary Zukav

Richard Barrett, vice president at the World Bank, thought of quitting his job. But before he could do that, he wanted to see what he could do about the lack of spirit there. Richard placed a note on the bulletin board, inviting those who were interested in pursuing the subject of spirit at work to join him in a brown-bag lunch. Forty people gathered that first day; within a year attendance was up to four hundred! The *Washington Post* wrote about it, as did the *Wall Street Journal*. In time, Richard did leave his job, but not before discovering the impact that a single individual could have at work.

To me, spirituality at work means invisible life sources that sustain our inner humanness. These life sources will vary depending on the individuals in a particular workplace. One office group had learned many of the principles of the Twelve Step program used in various recovery circles. They placed a box labeled "God's Box" in an office file drawer. Quite a few employees wrote on slips of paper what they needed to let go of and dropped it in "God's Box." These employees had found a way to connect with and strengthen their spiritual life at work.

Just for today, I will honor my spirituality at work. What form will it take? Perhaps a few quiet moments for reflection, or meditation, or a journal entry. Or it may simply be revealing a part of myself to someone else.

February 16 ⌒ *Forgiveness*

"True forgiveness includes total acceptance."

—Catherine Marshall

When was the last time you chose to forgive someone at work? Perhaps it was you! Sometimes vivid stories remind us of the importance of forgiveness. As a guest on a television talk show, I was to speak on forgiveness. The main guest's daughter and mother had been killed in a car accident caused by a drunken driver. To my surprise, the driver appeared on the show as well. The main guest, still in deep grief, had decided to reach out to the driver; she knew the woman must be in despair. She was right; following the accident, the woman driver had locked herself in her basement, wanting to kill herself. The two women joined in asking for and giving forgiveness. It seemed miraculous, and yet genuine. Forgiveness matters; it stretches our capacity for compassion and calls for our acceptance of humanness, calling forth our highest self. The talk show host, Oprah Winfrey, sat in tears with the rest of us. We all had a memorable story of how forgiveness heals.

Just for today, I will ask myself whom I need to forgive; perhaps it is myself. I will take the next step and have the courage to ask for forgiveness.

"Selficide is the death of the self by standing still. . . . It is inertia."

—Tom Malone

Surely we know the devastation of suicide, but how much do we really know about the "other" death—the death of the self by standing still? Sometimes people get "stuck" in their relationships at work. They seem to practice rote behaviors. Not long ago, I met a man who was in "selficide." He was not suicidal, but he was frozen—stuck. Words of encouragement did not work with him. He did not appear to be depressed. It did not help when his boss gently threatened him. No approach seemed to have an impact. He closed his office door and sat listening to music with his earphones, supposedly working. Eventually he lost his job; this did shatter him.

Often it takes a shattering, dramatic move for us to awaken. We seem to fall apart, and perhaps that is how our heartminds can open to new pathways. Have you ever looked back on your own life to see how you became unstuck at a particular time? We often feel "unglued" while we are becoming unstuck, but that, too, is part of the spirit wakening.

Just for today, I will focus on doing something different at work—interrupt a pattern or take a risk. I will not experience selficide if I stay awake to all the opportunities that surround me.

February 18 ⌒ *Compulsivity*

"When you can't control when you start it; when you can't control when you stop it . . . that is compulsivity."

—Harvey Milkman and Stanley G. Sunderwirth

Have you ever struggled with a compulsive behavior? Or wondered whether you were addicted? Not all compulsive behaviors are addictions. Many people who have grown up in shame-bound families have compulsive behaviors unrelated to physical dependency. Compulsive behaviors can be secret (eating disorders, cybersex, or overexercising) or very public. Workaholism, for example, has become the norm in many firms—workaholics' abnormal standards often result in promotions—yet this is a form of compulsion. Regardless of their form, all compulsions block our spiritual growth—this is why breaking free from such behaviors is so critical.

The first step in breaking compulsive behaviors is to name them. Then we can face our history of shame. Compulsivity has its own cycle. The shame that is kept alive through the compulsive behaviors serves to maintain the system. Often, people with compulsive behavior make promises to themselves and rely on willpower; we know that this is not enough. We need to go back and find the historical base for the behavior: What need was the compulsion born out of? What was going on in our family when we began the behavior? What pain were we trying to avoid? By answering these questions, we are moving forward on our spiritual journey.

Just for today, I will name my compulsive behaviors. I will seek support from others to help hold me accountable to change these behaviors and to identify their origins.

"A ship in port is safe, but that's not what ships are built for."

—Grace Murray Hopper

When we take risks, we are finding another way to reveal what we value in life. How can we learn—or act on our values—if we don't take risks? What would a risk in your workplace look like? Would it be asking for a raise? Would it mean giving feedback to a peer or superior? Would it mean saying no to a common rumor running through the organization? Or, perhaps, would it mean walking away from a gossip circle? What is risk for one is not for another. An act becomes a risk when we do not know the outcome. We are stepping into the unknown; we cannot see what the next step will be. Sometimes we realize we are standing still and if we do not take a risk, we could enter into inertia. We do not take risks for risk's sake, but rather when we know that we have a strong need for change. When we respect ourselves enough to risk, we are also enlivening our spirit by acting on our values.

Just for today, I will ask myself what I would lose if I took a risk. I will commit to taking the risk after thinking it through.

February 20 ⟡ *Letting Go*

"It's an invitation to cease clinging to anything—whether it be an idea, a thing, an event, a particular time, or view, or desire."

—Jon Kabat-Zinn

Often we do not realize what letting go really means. Have you heard the story about holding sand? When we cling and grasp tightly, not only does the sand escape, but we ache from the energy of holding on. Yet when we open our hand, the sand remains. Too often we live under the illusion that we control what is happening. When we struggle with problems, we grasp more firmly, get emotional about an issue, and work even harder at managing the outcome. We rarely see how invested we are in the process. When we let go and recognize that we are not likely to change anyone else's behaviors, we can trust that there are more life forces at work in a situation than our individual efforts. When we intentionally let go, we become open to new discoveries and can rest in the present moment and feel life fully.

Just for today, I will examine the corners of my life where I need to let go. I will allow these issues to come fully into my awareness, hold my hand (my mind) open, and see what comes with the gift of letting go.

"A kind and compassionate act is often its own reward."

—William J. Bennett

Can you think of the last time someone, through some action, showed compassion for you? Or the last time you showed your caring for someone at work? Compassion requires that we think outside of ourselves and focus on someone else's needs. It could be an offer to help an overworked colleague, or perhaps an empathic statement to someone who is suffering pain of any kind. Rod, a manager in a manufacturing firm, was greatly stressed and briefly mentioned to his superior that his teenage son was in trouble. Rod blamed himself; he knew his travels were out of control. Rod's superior immediately told Rod to stop all travel for the next two months and take time off to get some family help. "We can stay in touch by phone; we can live without you for a few months. This is not only your future, but your son belongs to our future." Rod was able to take advantage of this act of compassion and voiced his appreciation clearly and humbly.

Just for today, I will explore areas where an act of compassion might be appropriate; in addition I will be grateful for the compassion given to me.

February 22 ～ *Being*

"Often we find ourselves acting as 'human doings' rather than 'human beings.'"

—Anonymous

To focus on "being" at work, we must allow ourselves to be present and focus on what life is bringing to us, moment by moment. No matter where we are, we can stay in the present. Throughout our workdays, it is important to be able to hold on to ourselves and be fully present—awake. One day when leading a work group, I felt intimidated. The group's leader was one of the nation's most respected experts in his field. His group held him in regard. This intimidated me. The group knew little about me; all they knew was that their leader had trusted me. When we took a break, I left the room and focused on my breathing, reminding myself that I only had to "be" me. From that point on, the group discussion flowed. By staying present and focusing on being me rather than on what I was *doing,* I was able to work with competence and heart. While this method is never 100 percent successful, it felt like a gift from the spirit.

Just for today, I will pay attention to just "being" present and avoid any self-talk messages that can interrupt.

"The pattern that connects is the pattern that corrects."

—Gregory Bateson

Through our ability to connect, we gain the capacity to correct. When management or leadership teams learn to connect with one another, they can pass it on through all levels of the organization. By becoming more human with one another, they begin to "correct" the system. Recently a survey showed that empathy was among the essential skills that prominent business heads found necessary to lead in the new century. When people learn to truly listen, they can take the next step to empathy—the bridge to connecting.

Warren Bennis, a leading business author, wrote about the "Great Training Robbery" of the 1980s, referring to the billions of dollars spent on training. These programs did not necessarily affect the system. When such money is used for training people in "connecting," such as in emotional intelligence (EQ), we will see outcomes that truly can correct a system, rather than fitting someone's organizational model.

Just for today, I will pay attention to the connections I have at work and will be alert to any changes that I can make to help bring us closer to "correcting" the system.

February 24 ⌒ *Stubbornness*

"There is no greater weakness than stubbornness. If you cannot yield, if you cannot learn that there must be compromise in life—you lose."

—Maxwell Maltz

Jane had given a fine quote by Rumi, the thirteenth-century poet and mystic, to her friend Maxine. It stated simply: "Out beyond ideas of wrongdoing and rightdoing, there is a field. I will meet you there." This came about after a group of friends who worked together had a heated discussion in their book club. Reactions were strong. Strong professional women, several held to their conviction about what they believed was the "right" interpretation. Their stubbornness, which served them well in other parts of their lives, was useless here. Jane let the book group members know how she felt discounted because of their lack of flexibility when she presented her interpretation. She sent them each a note with the Rumi quote on a note card. Maxine was touched; she hung it in her study.

Stubbornness can be the downside of extreme loyalty to our beliefs. Yet loyalty and stubbornness walk a fine line. When we cross over into stubbornness, it can injure our relationships. We are then seen as unyielding and other people can give up on us.

Just for today, I will ask myself in what corners of my world am I stubborn? Can I put that stubbornness to work for a good cause where it can truly do good and not harm?

"The only thing we need to fear is fear itself."

—Franklin Delano Roosevelt

When fear arises, we typically find a defense for protection. Many of our fears, however, are phantom fears. They are fears without a real basis; they often are linked to an early life experience, not the present situation. Often we see fear governing a workplace. We see fear caused by intimidating leadership, surprise changes with downsizing, or disrespectful management. Some of these fears might be rightly justifiable, but many of the fears are our own phantom fears and can be a hiding place for those of us who fear change. Fear can also give us that edge of excitement in our lives, igniting our spirits. Bobby McFerrin, who had committed his work life to music, had an awakening when performing one night. By the time he had won eight Grammy Awards, he said that when he stepped out onto the stage, his fear was gone. He knew the value of the "edge" of excitement that comes from fear; he thus made a career move and became the creative chair of the St. Paul (Minnesota) Chamber Orchestra.

Just for today, I will ask myself where my real "edges" are in my life. I'll also ask which fears are real and which are phantom.

February 26 ～ Daring

"To dare is to lose one's footing momentarily. To not dare is to lose oneself."

—Søren Kierkegaard

When was the last time you dared to speak your truth when treated disrespectfully? Or perhaps you said no to a powerful person—a bold confrontation. To confront boldly does not mean disrespectfully; it only means that you know the truth. When we are awake, we are in touch with the opportunities to dare that present themselves. In a seminar, I asked a group of women to break into smaller groups and talk about their daring moments—when they dared being true to themselves at work. Afterward, each table selected a story to share with the entire group. We heard inspiring stories of women standing up. One woman stood up to a senior executive's come-on. Another woman walked away from a group of men telling off-color stories; these men had the power to promote her. We were all fascinated to learn, of course, that no woman was fired for her daring. The seminar participants also knew that they gained more of themselves by daring.

Just for today, I will dare to speak my truth. I will honor staying with the truth that has been growing in me through the years.

"Her back ached with the burdens other people were carrying."

—Hilda Lawrence

Often we are very good at empathizing and feeling the burdens of others. But how do we handle *self-*empathy? If we are going to maintain, or gain, a strong sense of self-esteem, we must be able to empathize with ourselves. Self-empathy is not self-pity; rather, self-empathy refers to our connection with the feelings from our own life experiences. We must be able to honor the young child who has lived within us—the child who didn't always know how to figure life out and perhaps made some unwise choices. This same child might have used emotional amnesia to survive painful memories. In self-empathy, we are honoring our reality, our true stories with all their feelings, no matter how long ago they occurred. This is very different from self-pity, in which one feels *for* himself or herself, rather than feeling *with* oneself, respectfully. When we can have self-empathy, we are better able to be with others in understanding where they are.

Just for today, I will acknowledge that I deserve self-empathy just as I deserve to empathize with others.

February 28 ⌒ *Play*

"You can discover more about a person in an hour of play than in a year of conversation."

—Plato

How do you play at work? Play can be a very constructive force in the workplace; it reduces stress. Once when working with a very serious group, I decided to approach their teamwork problems in a little different way. Separating the group into subgroups of eight, I gave them the following directions: "In a circle, with your right hand, grab the right hand of a person across from you.... Then with your left hand, take the left hand of a person across from you ... not the same person. ... Then get out of the knot." The groups laughed while playfully competing to complete the task. They had to communicate with one another, and we heard much laughter as they unknotted themselves. Afterward, while people were still in an energetic state, we "processed" what had happened. We asked how they solved their problem, what constituted good problem solving, and what had made their team successful (or not). The groups were surprised to discover how much relevant learning came from their "play."

Just for today, I will ask myself how I can bring a sense of play to work. How can I bring a smile into my workplace?

Sincerity ⌒ February 29

"The most exhausting thing in life is being insincere."

—Anne Morrow Lindbergh

What do you think of when you think of sincerity? Recently, a man told me how very exhausting it was to keep up his image. Tall, white-haired, and appearing very confident, he impressed people readily. Yet he knew he was in trouble; he was very engaged in "image management"—that is, managing his behaviors and appearance to convince others to respect him. Because of this investment, he was quite surprised when he received feedback from customers that he just wasn't sincere. He would have received an A plus in politicking, insincerely telling others what he thought they wanted to hear. It did not take too long for him to be found out. His insincerity came from low self-esteem and a fear of failure, of not trusting himself. When he decided to start speaking from his heart, while still fully aware of possible consequences, he found it better to be silent than insincere. He is now getting feedback from others about how much more believable he is; he is now gaining, not losing, customers.

Just for today, I will speak from my heart. Rather than speaking politically, I will either voice my convictions honestly or remain silent, thus being true to myself.

March

"Shame is the most powerful motivator of human progress."

—Yevgeny Yevtushenko

Do you know what motivates you? Do you know whose flames you have ignited? Motivating others is indeed like lighting another's candle. There are two types of motivation. The first, negative motivation, comes from attempting to escape shaming parental messages that told us "You will never be as good as your brother!" or "We always hoped that you would have become a doctor, not a secretary!" Such shaming messages drive us to move far from the internalized shame. In this example, we see people motivated to prove themselves. This can lead many to workaholism, a hiding place to escape their feelings. The second type of motivation comes from within, from our own values. Once, I asked a group of businesspeople to describe what motivated them. Their answers came promptly: The entire group spoke of their family commitments and their desire to make a difference in the world. This reminded me of the connection between healthy motivation and spiritual growth.

Just for today, I will honor my spirit and ask myself what comes from within me, my own inner voice, to motivate me in my work. I can choose to lead from within.

"Honesty without sensitivity is brutality."

—Anonymous

Just how honest can you be at work? Our roles and status and peer work relationships can often keep our truth telling in check. What are the consequences of being honest? Some people have an attitude of "this is for your own good" in giving honest and hurtful feedback. "I knew you would want to know about this. . . ." can sometimes be devastating to the recipient. When we are honest with another, we must ask ourselves what our intentions are. "Is this truly for the receiver, or is it for me to feel superior?" We must be sensitive to the other person—this means asking ourselves whether he or she is ready to hear the feedback, whether the timing is good, and whether we have a relationship in which the feedback can be heard. If you want to learn something about your spiritual growth, create a time line of instances in which you risked genuine honesty. Then next to each incident, write the consequences of your sharing and the feelings you experienced afterward. This exercise can demonstrate the benefits of honesty.

Just for today, I will be honest and sensitive. Sometimes it is important for me to be honest with myself and my observations and choose not to share them at work.

"Your I.Q. will get you your job; your E.Q. will help you keep it."

—Daniel Goleman

One of the nation's most brilliant scholars became a businessman. He was extremely intelligent and had received many honors throughout his life. His social skills, however, would have given him a failing grade. He was insensitive to others, had almost no self-awareness of his behaviors, and had never experienced empathy. He was truly "filled up with himself." While his IQ was extremely high, his EQ was dismal. He did not see why he would need any coaching; he thought other people did not understand how to deal with him. He eventually left the business world.

Psychologist Daniel Goleman researched what it is that makes people truly successful. He found that their emotional intelligence was the major factor. EQ, as he calls it, includes self-awareness and impulse control, persistence, zeal and self-motivation, empathy, and social deftness. Howard Gardner, the Harvard visionary who writes about eight types of "smart," argues that there are hundreds of ways to succeed and many different abilities that will get us there.

Just for today, I will pay attention to the wholeness of my intelligence. I will recognize that I possess a multitude of competencies and gifts and many abilities to help me become truly successful.

March 4 ～ *Regulating Boundaries*

"Motivation is usually when your dreams put on work clothes."

—Benjamin Franklin

Do people in your workplace treat your personal space with respect? One metaphor that often helps people better understand boundaries is a picture of a large capsule of fine mesh, or screenlike material, that contains three circles—the intellectual self, the emotional self, and the physical self. The capsule is the personal boundary that protects the self. Next picture two zippers on the capsule—one on the inside and the other on the outside. If one's boundaries were violated or ignored in childhood, we are vulnerable to others "unzipping" our boundaries and invading us. If our boundaries were respected early on, we can regulate our zippers from within and thus protect ourselves. When a CEO, in a company seminar on boundaries, asked a subordinate why he took such distance from her in the exercise, he looked at her, astonished, and said, "Why, that's simple—you're the CEO!" Ethnicity and status affect how we regulate our boundaries. With our boundaries intact we provide space for our spirit.

Just for today, I will pay attention to regulating my boundaries and pay attention to the boundaries of others.

"Somewhere along the line of development we discover what we really are and then we make our real decision for which we are responsible. Make that decision primarily for yourself, because you can never really have anyone else's life not even your child's. The influence you have is through your own life and what you become yourself."

—Eleanor Roosevelt

Empowerment certainly has a positive tone, but this term is often fuzzy in definition. What do we mean by empowerment? We see empowerment in who is legally authorized to do what and in what role. In the workplace, we see it in defined roles. But the true empowerment is seen in self-actualization, our natural ability to act in our own and others' behalf. We gain empowerment when others believe in us—it can come from peers, parents, partners, and friends. It can also come from a social movement, such as the women's movement or the Adult Children of Alcoholics movement. Empowered, we take our lives in our own hands. We are in charge of our own lives and our decisions, based on our own values. This is primary to our spiritual development. Often we can empower others simply by delegating some project to them, showing that we believe in them. When a work culture is committed to change, it can empower employees to take individual responsibility.

Just for today, I will ask myself my own areas of empowerment and focus on how I can work toward empowering a peer at work.

March 6 ⁓ *Being a Leader*

"You can teach what it is; you can teach how to do it. You can never teach how to be it."

—Carl Whitaker

To be a leader means that we convey our messages from the inside out. Being a leader means that we allow our authentic selves to be seen and known. Often people assume that someone is a good leader because of a job title; yet the real leader might be someone without a high-ranking title, a "natural" leader. Centuries ago, Socrates wrote, "May the inward and outward be as one." Being a leader means that we can take risks, make mistakes, and allow the same for others. We ask the questions, "How congruent am I in my behaviors? Do I 'walk my talk'?" But being a leader means that we also know how to follow. An article in the *Harvard Business Review* entitled "Why Should Anyone Be Led by You?" describes four characteristics that make an exceptional leader: revealing yourself appropriately, being unique in some expression of yourself, practicing "tough empathy," and using intuition. What kind of a leader are you? Who follows you? In what contexts?

Just for today, I shall focus on "being" a leader in the various ways in which I lead. And I will pay attention to how I follow.

"There is no change without loss."

—Harry Levinson

Renowned psychologist Harry Levinson says that corporations need to grieve their losses. Much of the dysfunction or "stuckness" in the workplace comes from the buried emotions of unresolved grief. How do we handle our feelings when a whole division of our company is shut down, moved to another city, or sold? How does this connect with previous losses in our lives? Many leaders in the field of addiction argue that unresolved grief lies at the core of addiction. It is important that we recognize our need to grieve—work losses as well as personal losses. When we acknowledge our personal and shared losses at work, rather than unknowingly dragging our loads of unresolved grief with us, we feel spiritually alive.

When a large computer parts company laid off thousands of workers, the company brought in professionals to hear their feelings and help the workers write resumes. This gave the employees an opportunity to both grieve and focus on a new beginning.

Just for today, I will reflect on my losses—both old and new—and allow myself to feel them.

March 8 ⌒ *Coping with Change*

"There is no sin punished more implacably by nature than the sin of resistance to change."

—Anne Morrow Lindbergh

Our rate of change today is exponential; change today is not what it used to be. At one time we viewed change comfortably—as within our control; it seemed continuous. Today we all see how the pace of change has been speeding up. A recent survey found that more than four out of five U.S. firms were in the midst of "major change," yet a Gallup/Proudfoot study in the same year found that more than half of the executives surveyed had doubts about their firms' abilities to address changes. Thus, we are all riding in the white water through the rapids of change. Many of us fear change in the workplace. In America today our largest private employer is Manpower Temporaries; we are facing changes in the workplace we never dreamed could occur.

How do you cope with change? Have you asked yourself what might contribute to your fear of change? We can usually find an answer there. Usually our resistance to change is the fear of going where we have never gone before.

Just for today, I will reflect on how I cope with change and recognize how much change I have already experienced in my life and survived so well.

"Stress is an ignorant state. It believes that everything is an emergency."

—Natalie Goldberg

Are you aware of how you cope with your work stress? Many studies show that up to 40 percent of workers report too much stress on the job. And 50 percent of these workers have a spouse they bring the stress home to. Stress is natural; it is what we do with the stress that makes the difference. Many of the changes common in companies today—increased responsibilities, promotions, and downsizing—affect the stress level of workers. Coping with stress requires intentional planning. Some people cope by assessing priorities; others practice meditation. Many learn that developing healthy behaviors in exercise, eating, and relaxation makes a difference. Others like to "decompress" by reading a newspaper, sitting in silence, taking a brisk walk, or "zoning out" with TV.

If we are blind to how stress affects us, we may injure our relationships with others. It is up to each of us to comment on our stress, talk with someone about it, and take responsibility for learning to leave the stress at work.

Just for today, I will focus on what my usual practices are regarding my stress. I will focus on the sources of my stress and explore new coping methods.

March 10 ∽ Listening

"The hearing ear is always found close to the speaking tongue."

—Ralph Waldo Emerson

Listening research shows that we hear only about 60 percent of what is said. This has nothing to do with the functioning of our ears; it has to do with paying attention. Listening is a learnable skill, but it requires focused energy. Not long ago, I met a woman who thought that her manager considered her boring because he seemed not to listen to her. But soon she recognized that his lack of attentiveness to what she was saying was about his rudeness—not about her personality. While our communication research shows that we have 6,000 words in our spoken vocabulary with 120,000 meanings, imagine how little we truly understand! To truly listen, we must face the speaker and focus on what he or she is saying to us and tune out all the internal "noise" in our heads. When we can truly hear one another, we are creating the possibility for connection.

Just for today, I shall listen attentively, to everyone, with undivided attention.

"Patience and time do more than strength or passion."

—Jean de la Fontaine

When was the last time that someone was impatient while you were attempting to complete something? How did you feel during that encounter? Often when we sense someone else's impatience, we become anxious and our tasks take even longer. But what about your own impatience? How do you handle that? Our impatience can certainly be a barrier to connecting with other people. When we display our impatience, people often feel as if they don't matter. When working with a family business not long ago, I found myself repeating my comments over and over to the eighty-four-year-old founder of the business. As I summarized and then re-summarized, he finally turned to me, undoubtedly sensing my impatience, and said, "I'm not 'getting it,' am I?" A man with a keen mind, he nonetheless had difficulties understanding the feelings that his children could express openly. At that moment, I broke into laughter and realized how foolish my attempt was to insist that he understand as fully the language of feelings as his much younger business partners. My impatience suddenly melted away and we were able to move on with our discussions.

Just for today, I will take a deep breath every time I feel impatient. I will ask myself what is stopping me from being present.

March 12 ～ *Harmony*

"You don't get harmony when everybody sings the same note."

—Doug Floyd

How do you experience harmony at work? We typically experience it through cooperation in projects or in meetings where everyone seems "tuned in" and can hear one another. When we are working in a cooperative environment, we have an opportunity to experience synchronicity at work. Synchronicity refers to the moments when there is a true sense of cooperation. We know that barbershop quartets as well as other music groups and athletic teams experience this. Of course they get to practice to achieve such harmony. When we give ourselves permission to be truly "with" our colleagues or co-workers, it becomes possible to tap the spirit in the workplace. The feelings of harmony send an energy into the air around us; we know that we are a part of the whole.

Just for today, I shall focus on cooperating with all those around me.

"To say, 'well done' to any bit of good work is to take hold of the powers which have made the effort and strengthen them beyond our knowledge."

—Phillip Brooks

When was the last time you genuinely praised someone for an accomplishment? It costs so little to give praise and yet can mean so much to its recipient. We surely know that when people are praised for work well done, they become motivated to work harder. When we are in a workplace that values praising one another, we often can *feel* the encouraged environment.

On the other side of giving praise, however, is receiving praise. My daughter used to say to me, when some recognition or honor occurred, "Let it in, Mom, let it in." She understood how hard it is to take what we so willingly give to others. Recently, a client of mine addressed a professional organization. He had put many hours into preparing for his talk, and it was received with a standing ovation. However, he was uncomfortable with this show of approval and had a hard time acknowledging it. Remembering my daughter's words, I turned to him and said, "Let it in, Doug. Let it in." He smiled, visibly relaxed, and said, "I am; I am." He was truly learning to balance his capacity to give and receive praise.

Just for today, I will pay attention to giving and receiving praise and ask myself which is easier for me.

March 14 ⌒ *Mastery*

"One can have no smaller or greater mastery than mastery of one's self."

—Leonardo da Vinci

Mastery is important to all of us. Mastery gives us a sense of self-esteem and confidence in an area of specific learning. Often we hear people complain at work that someone is not motivated. When one has a sense of mastery in a given area, that person will be self-motivated and will not need to turn to someone else for inspiration. Recently, someone asked me if I could "coach" a worker named Ned. While Ned was very bright, he did not shine in his position as his employer was sure he could. With the human resources director in the plant, Ned's supervisor set up a set of experiences in which Ned could gain incremental successes. He then built on his previous competencies and developed the mastery that was needed in his work. Within a few months' time, Ned was not only highly productive but also exhibiting a different, more positive sense of himself. By his self-motivation he became a model for his co-workers and the energy in his division gradually became more positive.

Just for today, I will ask myself what I have mastered and what I would like to master.

"We must walk consciously only part way toward our goal, and then leap in the dark to our own success."

—Henry David Thoreau

How do you know when you have been successful in your work? Sometimes you may not *feel* successful at all; in fact, you might be feeling just plain weary. For many years Al Bandura, a renowned psychologist from Stanford, has been studying "efficacy"—our belief in ourselves to make things happen. Efficacy is very important to our success. The other half of the success factor is that, along with goals, we must have feedback. When we set clear goals and meet them, and also receive trustworthy feedback, we see high success.

A few years ago I worked with a man, Josh, who was about to be promoted. But first, Josh had to change some behaviors; Josh had not received much constructive feedback throughout his career at the company, however. His supervisor asked for feedback from his peers and his subordinates and when Josh saw the feedback, he was grateful. He then set about to make the changes and within six months received the promotion. Early on, Josh had the motivation to succeed, and when he received feedback, the other critical ingredient to success, he was on his way.

Just for today, I will see where I can give some genuine feedback to someone who has fulfilled a goal. I will also ask for feedback about my own efforts.

March 16 〜 Blame

"The degree to which you blame is the degree to which you're stuck in your family [of origin]."

—Merle A. Fossum and Marilyn Mason

It is always obvious when we hear little children say it. "It's not my fault—it's his (or hers)!" But how do you handle those occasional chronic blamers at work? Blaming is an indicator that someone is caught in "invisible loyalties" to the family he or she grew up in. Perhaps it was not safe to take responsibility for what happened at home; maybe we had angry or hostile parents and feared owning our behaviors because of harsh punishment if we did. Blaming may also be a result of sibling relationships, as some children use their young age or their small size to place blame on a bigger or older brother or sister. These same patterns are often carried unconsciously into work. When people attempt to blame someone else, they are not taking responsibility for their part, however small, in what has gone awry. Have you ever observed your own blaming? I have sometimes had to laugh at my own tendency to blame when I am behind a slow driver while en route to the airport. Of course I blame the driver rather than take responsibility for my not leaving home early enough.

Just for today, I will observe whether I have blaming tendencies and I will search for any beliefs from my past that could contribute to my own blaming.

"Trust your hunches. They're usually based on facts filed away just below the conscious level."

—Dr. Joyce Brothers

How often have you said to yourself, after going ahead with something that turned out all wrong, "I knew I should have listened to my gut; I *knew* something was not right!"? Often we say we have hunches or instincts that tell us in what direction we should move—or not move. Since intuition does not come from the brain's logic center, too often it is easily dismissed. Suzanne Langer, a philosopher, said that intuition is the highest form of knowing. Aristotle even said that intuition is the source of scientific knowledge! Intuition is the most ancient form of knowing. Often we can make our best decisions if we can listen to what some call our "gut knowing." I know that sometimes my intuition leads me, and I have to give a "no" without having all the reasons. I recall working with a group of businesspeople who learned to use their intuition in the business planning meetings; it was most unusual to sit in with them and hear them say, "My hunch is that . . . and I will find the data soon." Using intuition does not mean that facts don't count; it simply means that we have a subconscious available to guide us if we choose to trust it.

Just for today, I will trust my "gut knowing" and see what results come. This may require me to take real risks; I will trust my intuition to guide me.

"Success without honor is an unseasoned dish; it will satisfy your hunger, but it won't taste good."

—Joe Paterno

When was the last time you were honored or recognized for a contribution you made at work? On the night of an annual recognition event to honor top producers, one firm did something different. This particular year a group of employees had gone to the CEO about a colleague they wanted to honor—Janice. Janice had made all the arrangements for the company-wide event. On the night of the event, a very weary Janice looked exhausted from all the preconference work. She was quiet during the dinner but suddenly heard the CEO call her name. Janice was a bit nonplussed; what was going on? She had done close to fifteen of these annual meetings and no one had ever asked her to come up front. The CEO made laudatory comments of appreciation and presented a lovely leather box "to hold some of the memories of all these successful events you have choreographed." Janice, overwhelmed, was able to give gracious words of acceptance. Janice felt a glow of renewed energy; she was recognized for her contribution.

Just for today, I will ask myself in what way I can honor someone else.

The Intangibles ∽ March 19

"The intangibles drive the tangibles."

—Harry Beckwith

More than ever, companies recognize that profits can be maximized by putting people first. Today 75 percent of Americans work in the service sector. Although their success is based on their relationships with customers, most of us could share numerous tales of poor service. However, some companies have learned that when they focus on the intangibles, all things are possible. Recently when a natural foods retailer came into town, it quickly became apparent that the company focused on service and employee satisfaction. There is always enough help available who have positive, helpful attitudes. One day, after an employee escorted me personally to the water cooler I was seeking, I asked him what he thought contributed to the positive environment in their store. He said, "When we all do well as a team, we are rewarded in many different ways, one of which is financial. We are appreciated." Now it would be difficult to measure statistically what the team's attitude consists of, and yet the store is constantly crowded. The positive intangibles are at work here and everyone wins.

Just for today, I will focus on how the intangibles of my workplace influence my working environment. Are the intangibles supporting or hindering our efforts?

March 20 〜 Curiosity

"Curiosity is, in great and generous minds, the first passion and the last."

—Samuel Johnson

Often at work, we hear people complain about being bored. Curiosity is the greatest antidote to boredom. Have you ever noticed that the curious people are also the most interesting? These are the seekers. Perhaps they question how things work, or perhaps they are curious to understand how a work system has come to be governed in the way it has. Curiosity is an energy force that keeps us feeling alive—the aliveness that tells us there is no room for boredom. I just spoke with a friend who has decided to take her work into an entirely different arena. Considered an expert in her field, she moved on, trusting her wisdom. She is curious to learn about the new multicultural group of people she will be working with. Her curiosity gave her energy to engage fully; it took her down her heart's path. Our curiosity allows us to understand more deeply, to do things differently, to create new learning curves for ourselves. I recall a group of executives in a high-tech firm that spent two full hours every Monday morning exploring what they were curious about; they knew the value of curiosity in a rapidly changing work environment and asked "out of the box" questions they were curious about.

Just for today, I will not cease questioning. I will ask questions I might not have been asking.

Enthusiasm ∽ March 21

"Enthusiasm is contagious. Be a carrier."

—Susan Rabin

Enthusiasm is contagious. It's like the Pied Piper—it is hard not to follow someone who is enthusiastic. Enthusiastic people are often natural leaders—their energy is inviting. Enthusiastic people look ahead; they do not dwell on the past or on what might go wrong. They look for what is going right and build on that. What is important to recognize is that unless you believe you can produce desired results, unless you have enthusiasm, you cannot move through the difficulties.

Recently, I walked into a work-group meeting and felt high energy in the air; the group members had been working on their vision and were reviewing all the possibilities they had named. The enthusiastic leader had engaged the entire group. Often in work seminars I ask people to tell the person next to them what they are most enthusiastic about at this time in their lives. This exercise quickly fills the room with energy. And this energy helps groups launch enthusiastically into the seminar content.

Just for today, I will ask myself what aspect of my job I am enthusiastic about. What is lifting my spirit today?

March 22 〜 Rewards

"Perhaps the reward of the spirit who tires is not the goal but the exercise."

—E. V. Cooke

What rewards do you receive for the work you do? How dependent are you on these external rewards? Or are you at a point in your life where you know that you are doing good work and that the rewards you receive are intrinsic, that is, they come from within? In an ideal world, we would not rely on external rewards. Our spirits certainly do not have that need, but often our egos do. Sometimes it is helpful to reward yourself for a job well done. One worker knew that her rewards were intrinsic but decided to give herself external rewards as well. She filled a jar with a list of rewards. Then upon completing a major task, she would dip into the jar and give herself a reward. It may have been a half hour of reading or a walk in the woods at the day's end. What is important to recognize is that, for some jobs, external rewards will not be extended. At times we need to take responsibility for rewarding ourselves.

Just for today, I will ask myself what rewards I seek and how I can reward the work of others and myself.

"Creativity is thinking up new things; innovation is doing new things."

—Theodore Levitt

Have you at times found yourself challenged by new ideas proposed in your workplace? Often people fear innovative ideas because they think any change will be permanent, regardless of its effectiveness. However, by redefining *change* to mean *experimentation,* we find that people are much more willing to accept change.

If you have an innovative idea, can you suggest that it be tried as an experiment for three to six months? After that time, the change would be evaluated honestly and may take hold or the system may revert back to its original form. Recently, a client concerned about employee retention decided to experiment with hiring practices. Rather than holding only in-office interviews, he decided to interview in three sites: office, restaurant, and candidate's home. This innovative idea dramatically shifted the kinds of observations as well as the kind of questions asked and over time improved the retention of employees. After a certain period, this approach became standard practice.

Just for today, I will focus on my attitude toward innovative ideas. I will be open to exploration of my own and others' ideas.

March 24 ～ *Truthfulness*

"You will never find yourself until you face the truth."

—Pearl Bailey

Being truthful is key to clearing the way for the spirit. When we know we are not truthful, we are clogging our spiritual energy lines. When we are truthful, we are honoring our own integrity and respecting others, knowing that they can hear the truth.

Joe was feeling bad about himself. He knew he was not facing the truth—that he was fearful of speaking up to his boss about the senior manager's lack of follow-through on team projects. The longer he hesitated, the lower his self-esteem plunged. Finally, Joe decided he had had enough; he took the risk and confronted his boss, illustrating his point with specific examples. The senior manager listened attentively and was surprised. He had had no idea how his behavior affected the team members. Others joined in and soon the group turned its attention toward new methods for timely completion of projects. Joe received high praise from the team as well as from his boss, and later, as a result of being truthful, he felt much more at peace with himself.

Just for today, I will be truthful, recognizing the risks of being straightforward with my opinions as well as the risks of living with dishonesty.

"People rarely succeed unless they have fun in what they are doing."

—Dale Carnegie

How do you have fun at work? Is your work environment one in which people can have fun while working hard at their jobs? A friend of mine works for a firm that believes in a fun workplace. Employees like to surprise one another. One day the company threw a surprise barbecue in the firm's parking lot with a live mariachi band. Just recently my friend told me that all but five of the three hundred employees attended another company-wide party at a local nightclub on a Saturday night. But the fun did not end that night; employees brought the fun-time energy into work early Monday morning as they reminisced about the party. A competitive spirit flames with the company's annual chili cook-off (and employees cannot register for the cook-off unless they have donated to the city's food shelf.) Another business group I work with includes "having fun while we succeed" as part of its mission statement. Clearly, these companies have learned that having fun fills their offices with high energy.

Just for today, I will ask myself what I can contribute to having fun in my work culture or to making it a fun place to work.

March 26 ～ *Self-Esteem*

"Think highly of yourself for the world takes you at your own estimate."

—Author unknown

Our work is a key source of our self-esteem; it is the place where many of our needs are met—or not. Since many of us re-create our family at our place of work, we are vulnerable to being treated by co-workers as members of our family of origin treated us. This treatment may mean improving or hurting our self-esteem, which is the source of our personal energy. Our connection to our colleagues and co-workers can affect both our self-esteem and our productivity at work. When our self-esteem is low, our ability to make confident contributions declines. In a state of high self-esteem, we can be creative, supportive, and productive.

Drs. Sid Simon and Howard Kirschenbaum used an acronym printed on a sign as a reminder of self-esteem: IALAC—I Am Loving and Capable. They illustrated that our signs can be torn by others, thus lowering our self-esteem. It is up to each of us to pay attention to our own IALAC sign and be mindful that we do not tear others'.

Just for today, I will pay attention to my self-esteem—when and how it is affected by the action of co-workers and how my actions affect the self-esteem of my colleagues.

"Forty-six percent of those who quit their jobs last year did so because they felt unappreciated."

—U.S. Department of Labor

Do you feel appreciated at work? We are human, and feeling appreciated is a basic human need. Often we assume that people know they are appreciated. Recently, I met with a group of senior managers who were shocked by the resignation of the company's star salesperson. "How can this be?" they asked. "Surely she knows we appreciate her." Unfortunately, however, their star employee did not feel that appreciation; they said it often among themselves but forgot to tell her.

Often, through the years, we can gain a sufficient sense of appreciation from within and from the outcomes of our work. However, when a young, high-potential leader is on the way up in a company, she or he might not yet have such a capacity. Self-appreciation develops with the experience gained through the years. Yet, for many younger people in search of good "work fits," appreciation from superiors is primary.

Just for today, I will appreciate being alive and knowing I am connected to a spiritual dimension of life, even through my work.

March 28 ~ *Wonder*

"A capacity for childlike wonder carried into adult life typifies the creative person."

—*Kaiser News Publication*

Many people would probably say that associating "wonder" with work is a contradiction. Not if we connect wonder with creativity, however. Yet, when we allow ourselves to wonder aloud in a safe setting, all things are possible. Can you let your mind imagine what can be? Albert Einstein, when creating his theory of relativity, did not use traditional scientific formulae. Rather, he created thought pictures which he shared with others and then thought through. He was using the right hemisphere of his brain, the side used to create vision and intuition. Using more fully the right hemisphere of the brain will help sustain a sense of wonder and instill creativity in our thinking. I recall one manager who said some of the best training he ever received was in studying jazz piano. Personal creativity can contribute to creative solutions to problems in the workplace and, thus, progress.

Just for today, I will allow myself to wonder, imagine, and create, knowing that it is going to help the whole.

"In solitude we become compassionate people, deeply aware of our solidarity in brokenness with all of humanity and ready to reach out to anyone in need."

—Henri Nouwen

Where can you find solitude at work? Finding a corner of solitude in the workplace can be very difficult. Some of us do not have office doors to shut. A woman I know makes sure she steps outside once each day and sits alone for a few minutes. Those ten minutes of solitude help her keep in touch with her feelings and the world around her. She needs to step outside in order to go inside.

Bill, a serious-minded senior executive, strives to be as mindful and alert as possible at work. Therefore, each day he takes fifteen minutes of his lunch hour and practices TM (transcendental meditation). He then returns to his full calendar and desk with renewed energy and a sense of peace. When we become still and can still our minds, we are ready to approach a stress-filled day with composure and awareness.

Just for today, I will find time to begin the practice of solitude, however short.

March 30 ～ *Uncertainty*

"The only thing that makes life possible is permanent, intolerable uncertainty; not knowing what comes next."

—Ursula K. Le Guin

Many have stated that the degree to which we can tolerate ambiguity is a key measure of our grown-upness. Ambiguity often results in feelings of uncertainty. Being able to live with uncertainty is key to our staying with our spirituality at work. Our spirituality often comes as a surprise; we cannot contrive a spiritual experience. Learning to live in the realm of uncertainty helps us know that we had better be careful not to have expectations set too high or to assume that things are going a certain way. Recently I observed that as the American workplace has continued to change dramatically, interest in spiritual growth and development has grown. Could it be that as workplaces become more uncertain, we have to turn to more fully living in the present? A woman I was doing leadership coaching with some years ago had a difficult time living with uncertainty, in and out of work. As she developed her spiritual practices, the dread of uncertainty started to fade. At the end of our work together, she told me, "I used to plan my life, and now I just show up."

Just for today, I will tell myself that I can join my spirit and not need to know what the future holds.

Confusion ∼ March 31

"It is only through disruptions and confusion that we grow, jarred out of ourselves by the collision of someone else's private world with our own."

—Joyce Carol Oates

I remember the first time I became lost when taking a business group on a mountain hike. I did not want to tell the group members that their leader was confused and lost. I stood still, in a state of confusion and controlled anxiety, and breathed deeply. I studied the setting sun, pulled out my compass, and checked my topographical map. Finally, I shared my confusion with the group, and after some discussion, we agreed on a return route and were soon back on our track.

It's not quite as easy to get back on track when I am feeling lost in my nonwilderness work; that is, lost *mentally*. On the trail, I had some simple tools—a map, the sun, and a compass. When options converge at work and jar our current thinking, I use the same tool of talking with others, but I also use the tools of writing notes to myself to clarify my thinking. Another tool I find helpful is ranking my alternatives. When I can know what my mind map holds, I am less likely to be confused.

Just for today, I will trust that my confusion is part of my path and remind myself of that truth.

April

"The first of April is the day we remember what we are the other three hundred and sixty-four days of the year."

—Mark Twain

Can you recall the last April Fools' joke that was played on you? And can you remember how foolish you felt for believing it? Could you tell others about it? Nobody knows for sure when the tradition of playing jokes on April 1 began. Some believe that it originated in the 1560s in France, when the king changed the new year to January 1. Some people didn't believe the change in the date, so they continued with the April new year celebrations. Others played tricks on them and called them the April fools.

When was the last time you were led to believe something false? Janeen received an e-mail stating that a competitive firm was buying her employer out; she in turn sent e-mails to about thirty co-workers telling them they had better "start looking" now. Within twenty-four hours, the original e-mail was clarified; there was no buyout. Janeen felt a little foolish as she sent out the corrected statement to her colleagues.

The humbling experience of life is recognizing that we will feel foolish at times. At work, this may mean that we will ask the wrong question or be totally confused when a co-worker or a superior tries to explain a new technique to us.

Just for today, I will allow myself to laugh at myself and some of my mistakes and misunderstandings, and I will share at least one with a good friend at work or with a family member.

April 2 ⌒ *New Beginnings*

"Again and again spring is here and not here."

—Bertha Damon

Spring is a time of new plantings and when dormant life reawakens. If we carry a "seasons" approach to life, we can keep the feeling/meaning of spring in our work by generating new ideas, turning new soil, and then planting ideas. To grow spiritually, we must recognize the importance of keeping springtime in our hearts. We don't have to let the calendar determine when we do our sowing. As with Mother Nature, all those germinated ideas will not take hold, but we can sow them anyway.

We often forget that we grow in darkness as well as light. John was highly distressed to learn he was being demoted. He had not produced in his role of senior sales director. Knowing, humbly, that he had misrepresented himself when hired, he decided to trust his superiors. John entered a mentoring program to learn the industry and narrowed his client load so he could succeed in one area. John truly created a spring for himself out of the darkness.

Just for today, I will assess where there is spring in my life and allow myself to sow some new seeds.

"He that always gives way to others will end up having no principles of his own."

—Aesop

Can you think of the last time you spoke your true voice? The voice is a gift; Longfellow called it the "organ of the soul." When we speak our true voices, we are speaking from the heart. Giving voice to something does not mean we have to blast it out at someone; often it is simply speaking that small voice within us that has been agonizing over whether or not to be heard.

Larry had been upset for a long time with his manager and with executive decisions at his company. He knew he had to speak up, yet he gave himself many excuses not to. Larry felt self-loathing about not using his voice; he was very clear when speaking to his close friends about the issues and often rehearsed silently what he wanted to say. When Larry finally took his stand, he was not only listened to but also received an invitation to attend monthly breakfast meetings where he could give additional feedback. Larry heaved a sigh of relief; his self-respect had restored itself.

Just for today, I will go within and ask myself what I need to give voice to. I will take the risk and speak up.

April 4 ~ *Higher Power*

"It doesn't matter what it is, as long as you ain't it!"

—Jo-Ann Krestan

Just what do we mean when we talk about our Higher Power? Our Higher Power may be part of a religious belief system, or it may not. For some, Higher Power refers to one's relationship with the natural world or to a combination of life forces. Our Higher Power is the source of our spiritual power, the energy we turn to when we are facing life's "edges." Our workplaces provide many instances when we need to call for some help.

The Twelve Step program states in its Second Step "that a Power greater than ourselves could restore us to sanity." When Edward faced a crisis at work after a consultant indicated that he had controlling behaviors, he knew he had to let go, but he didn't know how. "But what do you mean—let go to whom, to what?" Edward's comment marked the beginning of his spiritual journey, exploring what in life was greater than him that he could turn to. Today Edward can chuckle about his early question.

Just for today, I will remember that my Higher Power is always with me. It is up to me to seek my Higher Power's support.

"Every seed destroys its container else there would be no fruition."

—Florida Scott-Maxwell

Few of us simply glide into maturity. Usually, life crises provide the necessary opportunities for growth and transformation. Yet like all of nature, our seed has to destroy its container (old assumptions and beliefs) in order for us to become more of who we can be.

I remember years ago, when going through a personal crisis of divorce, I felt as if I had a plunger pulling on my brain. How could I do my work—my teaching—when I felt that all was falling apart around me? Sure, I had read about the promise of the "gift in the crisis," but I felt no sense of a coming "gift" at that time. I had been stuck and, working through it, I felt as if I was truly coming unglued. Yet in the process, I was breaking barriers, changing beliefs, and becoming more aware.

Even when change is good, it can be hard. What helped me was learning to ask for support while recognizing that change and growth are a part of life's process. I turned to my personal board of directors for the support I needed.

Just for today, I will let myself trust life and know that as my "edges" are pushed, I am in the process of becoming.

April 6 ~ *Deception*

"All deception in the course of life is indeed nothing else but a lie reduced to practice, and falsehood passing from words into things."

—Robert Southey

Have you ever experienced deception in your workplace? Hard as it is to believe, deception occurs all too often and costs businesses millions of dollars.

Recently, Jacqueline called, not knowing how to handle Hope, who lied in a meeting. Hope had seemed vengeful toward Jacqueline ever since she was hired for a position Hope had wanted. When a senior executive was governing his first meeting in the company, Hope, who was competing for department funding, lied about sales figures. When Jacqueline questioned Hope, which as Hope's superior was her responsibility, Hope replied, "So, you are calling me a liar!" Jacqueline felt devastated.

How do you handle such unprofessional behavior in a work setting? Jacqueline remained firm; her inner quivering did not show. She calmly stated that she was simply asking for the source of Hope's data because no one else seemed to have seen it. Jacqueline realized that Hope's behavior pattern was beyond her control; all she could do was stay with her own truth.

Just for today, no matter the behavior of others, I will stay with my own truth and be true to my own values.

"When the will is ready, the feet are light."

—A proverb

In researching some quotes on will and willpower, I was surprised to see how forceful the statements were, referring to "indomitable willpower," "domination," and "failure." Surely willpower is necessary for a strong mind-set in reaching our goals, but willpower in itself is not enough.

When I led a group of executives on a rock-climbing retreat, we all received a powerful message to be taken back into the workplace. When we used our concentrated willpower and determination, we often had bloody hands and knees from repeated will-driven attempts. We would fall and then use even more force and determination to climb a little higher, becoming more exhausted as we climbed. But when we learned how to balance our willpower with surrendering to the process of climbing, we saw new routes up the rock and climbed with an ease that will alone never allowed.

We all have our climbs at work. Our wills won't get us through, but our spirits will.

Just for today, I will recognize that my willpower must be balanced with my ability to surrender and let go, taking me in the "right" direction.

April 8   ~   *Expectations*

"Life . . . it tends to respond to our outlook, to shape itself to meet our expectations."

—Richard M. DeVos

It is natural to have expectations; our achievements have everything to do with our expectations. They can become self-fulfilling prophecies. While our personal expectations are often unspoken in our work lives, it's best to communicate expectations. Problems often result when co-workers have different but unspoken expectations.

Sara, a very successful career woman, had a positive attitude and high expectations of herself—"inner expectations" that served her well. Her "outer expectations"—her high expectations of others in her work group—caused her stress; she thought everyone else shared her expectations. One day, an office friend suggested she check out her group's expectations. As they went around the group, Sara was amazed to hear how different the expectations were. By addressing the differing expectations, the group was able to agree on a set of shared expectations and became much more efficient. This became a ritual in their group meetings. In time, not only did attitudes improve, but productivity did as well. Sara was also able to take her "discovery" and ritual home.

Just for today, I will check out my expectations of others and also monitor my expectations of myself.

"Perfect virtue is to do unwitnessed that which we should be capable of doing before all the world."

—François de La Rochefoucauld

The word *virtue* has often been characterized by "goody-goody" or "suffering in silence." Today, however, we know the importance of reexamining the role of virtue in our lives. Most of us have heard about the seven virtues that were passed on by Saint Thomas— faith, justice, hope, prudence, temperance, fortitude, and charity. These virtues recently received high acclaim through a documentary by Deborah Boldt. She filmed the work of a fresco artist who painted the virtues on a ceiling at Saint Thomas University in Saint Paul, Minnesota. Boldt interviewed everyone from heads of organizations to street kids about virtue and was more than pleasantly surprised to discover that people from all walks of life practice these virtues in their everyday work lives.

Virtues can become habits of moral excellence and goodness. Most of us know of workplaces where the Big Seven are supported. Usually people who are "walking their talk" do not use the word *virtue;* they simply live their well-developed habits of doing the right thing.

Just for today, I will remember the words of Martin Luther King Jr.: "The time is always right to do what is right."

April 10 ⌒ *Mistakes*

"Mistakes are the usual bridge between inexperience and wisdom."

—Phyllis Therous

How do you handle your mistakes? Do you beat yourself up for five years or are you able to forgive yourself and move on? Making mistakes is natural, and our spirits demand that we be forgiving. Our history often affects how willing we are to forgive ourselves. If you were humiliated or berated when you made mistakes as a child, for example, you will likely carry shame scars.

John, a factory supervisor, was not aware of how hard he was on his workers. He yelled at them when they made mistakes and created a fear-driven factory floor. Yet, costly mistakes, as well as numerous safety violations, continued to occur. Finally, John sought help for the problem. With a consultant's guidance, John looked at his own history and saw where he had learned his shaming behaviors. With this knowledge, John was able to own his own mistakes and, just as important, give others permission to make mistakes and to forgive themselves. This change slowly created a very different work culture—one that not only allowed mistakes but also experienced fewer safety violations.

Just for today, I will remember that I am truly human. I am a mistake-maker and a good person.

> *"Your brain is capable of handling 140,000 million bits of information in one second, and if you take hours or days or weeks to reach a vital decision, you are short-circuiting your most valuable property."*

—Jerry Gillies

How would you describe your decision-making ability? Do you need a lot of time for deliberation, or can you make decisions without an overload of information? Sandy was a well-respected employee in a high-tech company, but she could not overcome her lifelong pattern of sitting on decisions. She would spend so much time gathering information before making a decision that it interfered with her other work.

When Sandy learned that this process was tied to her fear of making mistakes, she acknowledged that she could never be perfect and resolved to change her behavior. She did this by setting deadlines for decisions and announcing those commitments to others. She cared more about her co-workers than herself in that decision, but it was the very motivation she needed. Within a few months, Sandy admitted that she did not have to be *that* deliberative. When she put aside her fear of making a mistake, she trusted herself enough to know she could make solid decisions even when she didn't have every fact and figure. She also became aware that this new way of working freed up mental and emotional time—a step toward freeing her spirit.

Just for today, I will focus on my decision making and center my energy on trusting when I have enough information.

April 12 ⌒ *Positive Energy*

"Go for the dry wood."

—Rene Schwartz

Have you ever felt as if you were beating your head against a concrete wall while trying to get something accomplished with some naysayers? You think that if you simply give enough reasons, others will come around to see things your way, but it just doesn't happen. Or, how many times have you found that you've invested energy in a Bank of the Bottomless Well that would pay no dividends for your invested energy?

Sometimes it's hard to accept that we are facing a very dead end and that despite the amount of energy we invest, nothing is likely to change—whether a work system or a co-worker or manager. When we "go for the dry wood," we can face the possibilities of igniting another person's spirit. When we pursue negative energy, on the other hand, it is like trying to ignite a piece of green wood. Imagine how we can kindle our own spirits when we know that we are influencing the spirits of others!

Just for today, I will ask myself whether I am focusing on positive energy, energy filled with possibilities and hope.

"No pessimist ever discovered the secret of the stars, or sailed to an uncharted land, or opened a new heaven to the human spirit."

—Helen Keller

Have you ever worked with a pessimist? Often these people cannot see the positive in anything. Martin Seligman, the author of *Learned Optimism,* argues that while pessimists might have the most realistic view of life, they are more likely to be depressed. Their pessimism is a self-fulfilling prophecy, for if we look for the negative side, it will usually be there. Have you ever tried to convince a pessimist that his or her views are tainted and that you can help by providing a clear vision? Your words fall to the ground; reason doesn't matter. The pessimist usually grew up with a negative parent.

Jeanette was a pessimist, as was her mother; she brought her negative energy into work every day. No matter how good the news at work, she always had a negative attitude and knew that "we'd better be suspicious." Jeanette eventually became isolated and lonely at work, thus reinforcing her pessimistic view of life. We can only imagine how discouraged her spirit must be!

Just for today, I will acknowledge that pessimists usually have stories involving deep hurt. Yet, I will not allow myself to be dragged into that swamp.

April 14 ⌒ *Long-Term Wins*

"If you want to have the rainbow, you gotta' put up with the rain."

—Dolly Parton

When we are in the midst of change, wondering whether the outcome will be what we planned, we often forget that rainbows come from rain. It's sometimes difficult to see the benefit of long-term projects when we live in a culture with so many instant rewards. With the efficiency available to us in today's world—cell phones, e-mail, personal computers, and microwaves—it's hard to delay gratification. Yet taking incremental steps can bring the rewards of long-term wins.

A financially successful company was concerned about all the female employees who had been leaving; retention issues were serious. "We just can't find women who are suited to this engineering work," the managers lamented. Still, they decided to do their best to solve the problem and began by examining their hiring process. After discovering that the process had become stiff and outdated, they implemented some changes. Younger men and women, who were asked to think more progressively, were called on to do the interviewing. They changed the questions to hone in on an individual's creativity and uniqueness and got to know applicants more intimately by interviewing for a longer period of time. Midstream they made further changes. Soon the company became known as "the place that is people friendly." Within two years they had overcome their retention issues. They saw the rainbow!

Just for today, I will remind myself that we cannot click into rainbows; we earn them!

"The ultimate measure of a man is not where he stands in moments of comfort and convenience, but where he stands at times of challenge and controversy."

—Martin Luther King Jr.

Where do you face challenges at work? Are you intimidated by certain people? Do you believe that you are supposed to have all the answers, even if you are new to your job?

What is a challenge for one is often not a challenge to another. When Elsie started her first job in the financial industry, she thought she would never be able to learn the vocabulary, let alone the methods used. She had strong people skills that covered her fear, but often these were misread as high competence. Her fear of being found incompetent was a daily concern. Then one day it clicked for her. When she and her boss made an all-day presentation, her new learning came together. At that moment, she knew she understood her work. She knew she was good enough, and she smiled—within and without. If we don't have challenges, how would we continue to grow and learn?

Just for today, I will accept that challenges are a true gift to my spirit. I will approach a challenge with anticipation and an open mind.

April 16 ⁓ *Thank-Yous*

*"If the only prayer you said in your whole life was 'thank you,'
that would suffice."*

—Meister Eckhart

Have you sincerely thanked someone today? Many people comment that thank-yous often sound insincere nowadays. While saying thank-you is certainly a polite expression, giving a sincere thank-you in whatever form can truly warm the heart. It may be through an e-mail message, a personal note, or even a surprise gift.

I recall working two long days and evenings with a group of businesspeople. These long hours were quite productive and resulted in some fine outcomes. Yet I put in more time than I had expected and even delayed my flight home by a day. Wearily, I entered my hotel room on the second night, intending to become "brain dead" for a few hours. On the table in my hotel room, to my surprise, was a lovely box of Belgian chocolates wrapped in a beautiful ribbon! A note was attached: "Thank you for your work with us." I was touched and warmed by the thank-you.

Just for today, I will express my appreciation for someone with a sincere thank-you.

"Few men during their lifetime come anywhere near exhausting the resources dwelling within them. There are deep wells of strength that are never used."

—Richard Byrd

In a perfect world, we have all the resources we need. But for many of us, this is not a reality—we lack the proper resources in people, equipment, or materials. It can be truly difficult to do work without the right resources, and it's a true challenge to our spirituality. At these times, we need to turn to our internal resources to create external resources. Limited resources can push us to think in new ways.

When one company learned how often employees were staying home to care for sick children who could not attend day care, they decided they had to act. Yet they simply could not afford to build an on-site child care center. After hours of brainstorming, they decided to provide their employees with backup child care in their own homes. Lo and behold, they suddenly had their "resources"—their employees—gratefully present and most pleased that they could allow their young sick children to stay at home. The creation of such a resource was a "win-win."

Just for today, I will examine my resources and see what inner resources I have to apply to my work world.

"Birds sing after a storm; why shouldn't people feel as free to delight in whatever remains to them?"

—Rose Kennedy

For most of us, the word *delight* would not pop into our heads when thinking about our workplaces. Yet if we look closely, we'll see that small acts that occur throughout the day result in delight. It could be looking out the window and seeing buds on a tree or spotting the first robin in the spring. Delight might also come as a surprise when we experience that almost childlike moment of joy for someone else's good fortune or from a job well done.

Have you ever noticed how delight moves through your entire body? Delight is like a warm massage throughout the nervous system. Delight is something we need to look for, or we will never find it. When we find true delight, our energy soars. And although delight is typically a brief interruption in a day, it reminds us that we bring our whole selves to work—our aesthetic selves, our heartful selves, and our aware selves.

Just for today, I will look for delight. I will carry the word in my line of vision so that I may see it clearly when it appears, in whatever form.

"Life is the first gift, love the second, and understanding the third."

—Marge Piercy

W hy is it so difficult to understand others some-times? Is it because we receive insufficient or in-accurate information about something? I have learned and relearned that when it is possible to take the time to hear someone's thinking—someone's perspective—on a subject, we can then truly understand. And when we understand, we can move toward acceptance of that per-son and his or her ideas.

Recently, I worked with a group in which one mem-ber was adamant about not spending another penny on development work or research, even though she knew it was essential. "We just cannot do that!" she said in a shrill voice. Hearing the emotional charge behind her words, I spoke with her privately and learned that at her previous company, an entire division had gone belly-up because of overspending on development and research. I wonder how often I make a judgment about someone's ideas be-fore I check out the underlying story.

Just for today, I will strive to understand. In areas that matter, I will attempt to learn the story behind the perspective.

April 20 ～ *Lifelong Learning*

"You should keep on learning as long as there is something you do not know."

—Lucius Annaeus Seneca

We do not stop learning when we receive our degree upon graduation. Rather, learning is a lifelong process. We are all learners, all of our lives, if we choose. Adult education courses have grown exponentially over the past decades. But whether in a formal or an informal classroom environment, we stretch our minds—and our spirits—when we pursue something new.

Thad learned that when he was feeling a little stuck in his work, it was time for another course in the arts. He took a jazz guitar class and found that it stimulated the right hemisphere of his brain and enhanced his general brain power. Suddenly, he could think clearly again—creative ideas arose almost daily. He knew that to have a full life, lifelong learning had to play a major role.

Just for today, I will ask myself how I am keeping my lifelong learning alive in my world. What captures my interest?

Miracles ∽ **April 21**

"I walk ahead of myself in perpetual expectancy of miracles."

—Anaïs Nin

What miracles have you witnessed in your life? Many of us would probably name the Berlin Wall coming down or the ending of apartheid in South Africa. But what about the little miracles that occur every day? If we look closely, we may see a true conversion of spirit.

One senior executive was known as "Grim Tim" in his firm. He seldom smiled. When Tim's boss asked him to work with a business coach, he learned how his co-workers viewed him. He recalled that when he was fresh out of business school, he noted that the older business executives did not smile, so he decided to adopt that behavior. (Ironically, he was called "Smiley" as a child.) Upon learning how he was perceived at work, however, Tim changed his behavior almost immediately. Soon thereafter, not only did others start seeing Tim differently, but Tim discovered that he felt quite differently toward others. People commented that they had witnessed a miracle.

Just for today, I will pay attention to the everyday miracles—the transformation of the spirit that may be occurring around me.

April 22 ~ Overkill

"The best things carried to excess are wrong."

—Charles Churchill

How much simpler life can be when we don't over-kill! Have you ever worked for a company that was determined to make a "cultural change" and impose it throughout the organization? Sometimes a plan handed down from the top can lead to resentful employees.

One organization decided to do something about its safety record; it did need improvement. A new manager was hired who set about raising the company's safety standards while also trying to carve a good name for himself. He implemented changes that were far beyond federal requirements. He required all workers at the auto parts plant to wear hair nets and white coats, even though many of these employees worked with dark-staining steel parts. The manager did not realize that he was insti-tutionalizing "overkill." He created policies for policies. He overlooked the fact that when employees have a high level of respect for and satisfaction with their co-workers, their safety record improves automatically; fewer accidents occur. He did not realize how his over-kill was stifling the spirits of the workers, who had become very negative and more prone to accidents.

Just for today, let me know where to draw the line and not become overzealous in attempting to make improvements. Enough will be just enough.

"Character is higher than intellect. A great soul will be strong to live as well as think."

—Ralph Waldo Emerson

What constitutes character? How do you know it when you see it? When I think of strong character, I think of my colleagues Marie and Josh. These two individuals are people with high principles and high standards. They treat themselves and others with a quiet sense of integrity.

Character never has to shout at us. Marie and Josh are humble. They display their character by controlling their emotions and by treating other people with respect and dignity. Our title or status in the workplace does not determine our character. Anyone, at any level of an organization, can have high character. Because good character does not manipulate, those with highest character often go unnoticed.

The workplace offers remarkable opportunities to shape character. At work, we often must decide whom we will stand up to and what we say no to. I believe that when we develop character, our ego-spirit also becomes balanced. As we're building our own character, it's often helpful to look for models of character in our world.

Just for today, I will ask myself what words I would use to describe character and ask myself how I am doing.

April 24 ∼ *Task—Getting It Done*

"Hell, there are no rules here—we're trying to accomplish something."

—Thomas A. Edison

Do you have people you can count on when you need to "get the job done"? During the hiring process, few references are asked how well they can implement or get the job done. The problem is often not discovered until a person is on the job.

"Getting it done" requires a can-do attitude. When people know how to cooperate and collaborate, they can usually get tasks done—on time! When Tony's deadline for completing an inventory was suddenly pushed up, he felt overwhelmed. He called his employees together, explained the task thoroughly, and asked for the group's help. They all pitched in, even skipping their regular hour dinner breaks and stopping only for short pizza parties. The group's dedication paid off—they finished the inventory one day ahead of schedule! Tony took the entire team out to a dinner on completion day. His enthusiasm and can-do attitude was contagious; he believed in his employees, and they believed in him.

Just for today, I will determine to "get it done" to the degree that it is possible. I will ask for help when necessary.

"You have to recognize when the right place and the right time fuse and take advantage of the opportunity. There are plenty of opportunities out there."

—Ellen Metcalf

So often I have seen people struggling to find their place, and they rarely know it is an issue. While a dedicated worker and cooperative team member, Sara had felt uncomfortable in her group's meetings and often sat through them in silence. When an employee from the communications department began working with Sara's division, he commented that she did not seem to take her place in their meetings. When he held a seminar on how early childhood learning is transferred to the workplace, Sara "got it." She was fascinated with her discovery that as the sixth-born of seven children, born just thirteen months after her brother, she had to squeeze into a chair at their crowded kitchen table. Her early years were difficult: her father was off fighting in Vietnam, and her mother was parenting alone with little money to spare. Sara was accustomed to feeling un-noticed. In her adult life, Sara had never thought about this. Once she knew the origins of this unintentional behavior, she was able to make changes immediately.

Just for today, I will recognize myself and know that I have a right to my place in this workplace, this world.

April 26 ⌒ *Confidence*

"You have to have confidence in your ability, and then be tough enough to follow through."

—Rosalynn Carter

Are you aware of what can threaten your confidence? Jack and Miriam moved fifteen hundred miles away from their families to fulfill Jack's career dream—a move that Jack had persuaded Miriam to support. When Miriam voiced her unhappiness and loneliness in their new town, Jack began to doubt his decision. His self-doubt soon seeped into his work; for the first time in his career, Jack's confidence in work-related decisions was waning.

Jack's employer said, "I don't think this is the Jack we hired; can I help?" Jack responded, "Thanks, I can take care of this. I know what to do." Jack then opened the long, hard conversations with his wife. By talking it through together, Jack and Miriam were able to find ways to give their lives in a new city a real try. As Jack shared his feelings of self-doubt with Miriam, his self-confidence returned.

Just for today, I will remind myself of my confidence and stay true to what I know. I will take care of any "unfinished business" that can erode my confidence.

"Anything more than the truth would be too much."

—Robert Frost

Have you ever told yourself that speaking the truth to "powers that be" in your work would lead to your dismissal? Fear prevents many from speaking out.

Jim, who worked in a medical setting, was shocked to learn that his program's director was going to lower the eligibility standards for new surgical procedures. These procedures could produce new revenue for the company, which was important in a tight health care market. Sleepless for many nights, Jim knew he had to speak his truth. He enjoyed belonging to this leading-edge medical group, yet he knew he must act. Jim, prepared to lose his job, met with the director and said what was on his mind. As Jim spoke steadily and calmly, his director was at first defensive. But when Jim was through, the director responded, "This took a lot of courage; I am impressed. I don't know if I could have done that at your age." The proposed change died at that point.

Just for today, I will speak truth to power. I will comment on my reality.

April 28 〜 *Persona*

"Nothing endures but personal qualities."

—Walt Whitman

Your persona is simply the inner qualities you possess that reveal themselves in your *role self,* or your "presentation" of yourself. Have you ever considered what you want your persona to be? If you want to become more of who you are, you must start by knowing yourself. Many people begin by "acting as if" until the desirable behaviors are integrated. As they make the behavioral changes, the inner self starts to shift.

Maria had been very frustrated with how she reacted to several senior male executives in her company. She was steadily working on changing her behavior, but progress came slowly. One day a friend suggested that she pretend to create a different persona—to act in role. Maria said, "Why not—I have nothing to lose! I probably couldn't have any more embarrassing moments if I tried!" Maria employed her new work persona, a self-description she had written out and carried with her. Before long, she had grown into the person she wanted to be.

Just for today, I will ask myself what kind of persona I want to grow into. I will remember that spirit grows when I shine from within.

Civility ⌒ April 29

"Politeness is the art of choosing among your thoughts."

—Anne-Louise-Germaine de Staël

To me, civility is a combination of politeness and consideration. No matter how others may speak or behave toward us, we can choose to behave with civility. We don't have to like co-workers or think of them as friends in order to treat them with civility. Every person deserves the attitude of civility in all messages.

I recall having to face a man who had betrayed the loyalty of a friend-colleague of mine. When I arrived to speak at a conference, I learned that my friend's nemesis was going to introduce me. I tightened up; my heart raced. My loyalty to my friend was strong! At first, I avoided the man but then determined that I would not let him control my feelings. I would stay with myself. I did feel anxious as I walked to the podium. He gave me a generous introduction, and I thanked him in a very civil tone. I felt calm and centered as I began to speak. Civility worked!

Just for today, I will be civil in all my interactions. I know that being my taller self feeds my spirit.

April 30 〜 *Goals*

"Man is a goal-seeking animal. His life only has meaning if he is reaching out and striving for his goals."

—Aristotle

Are you a goal setter? Do you like to map where you are going and determine how you'll measure your arrival? Goals can be a guide. They help us build our self-esteem as we enjoy the rewards of an accomplishment. Yet goals can also constrict, destroying spontaneity, if the focus is too narrow.

When I found myself far behind in my writing plan for this book, I spoke at length with Iris, a friend with whom I have a pact to "stay on the path." I felt guilty that I had fallen behind and knew I had to set a deadline goal for my publisher. My friend Iris took my hand and said, "Okay, repeat after me. 'I pledge . . .'" I then pledged aloud that I would have the book completed by a certain date and that I could set intermediate goals as well. While the decision and the goals were mine, it helped to have the support of a friend who promised to prompt me as I moved on my "path." I relearned the need to have support for my goals.

Just for today, I will ask myself what my goals are. I know how important it is to live with direction in my life.

May

"Good timber does not grow with ease; the stronger the wind, the stronger the trees."

—J. Willard Marriott

How do you handle adversity—strong differences and hard times? Some people fear adversity to the degree that they avoid numerous situations and thus block their spiritual growth. We often see patterns in how people handle adversity. Some totally avoid the hard stuff; others seem to thrive on such a challenge. Still others are able to face adversity with a steady calmness.

In his book *Adversity Quotient*, Paul Stoltz discusses the patterns we use in facing adversity. He identifies three distinct roles people take when faced with adversity: the Quitter, the Camper (someone who sits still), and the Climber. Stoltz's findings reveal that how we face adversity determines our success. Recently, I worked with a team in which the leader so feared adversity of any kind that he bent toward anyone who showed the slightest irritation with him. As the team focused on how they faced adversity in their lives, however, this man gradually became a strong leader.

Just for today, I will face adversity with head and heart. I will not let my history block my growth.

May 2 ⁓ *Learning from Disappointments*

"You may be disappointed if you fail, but you are doomed if you don't try."

—Beverly Sills

Life has some guarantees for us, and one is that we will face disappointment.

Nick was a loyal, dedicated factory employee who had always thought he would be the natural replacement for the division manager. Shortly after the manager's departure, the management team announced that a person from the outside had been hired as division manager; Nick's heart sunk. Upon hearing the news, he could hardly face the heavy disappointment he felt and worked hard to control his tears. Anger followed the disappointment. He considered leaving, not trusting that he could work for the new manager and still be productive.

After sharing his story with some good friends, Nick realized that he had never made his hopes and expectations known. Nick walked through his work life with unstated expectations. Many of us do this. We think, "If you care about me, you will . . ." Such expectations can bring sore disappointments.

Just for today, I will check my assumptions and expectations to ward off unnecessary disappointments. I will practice sharing my expectations.

Defeat ⟜ May 3

"You can learn a line from a win and a book from a defeat."

—Paul Brown

How have you experienced defeat in your life? In political elections or in sports, or in competing for a job, the defeats are clear. Yet many defeats are not visible to others because a goal was private and unspoken or the competition was underground. As adults, we often struggle with defeat. We feel entitled to a promotion or deserving of a raise. To protect ourselves from feelings of failure, we blame others when we are defeated.

When rock climbing with young children some years ago, I noticed that when they were "stuck" on the rocks and could not go forward, they simply said, "It looks like this is not working; I had better try something new." They seemed to have no ego attachment with defeat or success. These children accepted that it is human to feel defeat. We need to remember this. Defeat is natural; we learn and grow from it. In many cases, success comes only after repeated failures.

Just for today, I will accept my defeats with my head held tall. I accept defeat as part of my humanness.

May 4 ～ *Pride*

"I am impelled, not to squeak like a grateful and apologetic mouse, but to roar like a lion out of pride in my profession."

—John Steinbeck

Just what is pride? Dictionaries define it with synonyms such as *arrogance, smugness, self-respect,* and *satisfaction.* Such opposing terms! Just how do *you* interpret pride? I look at pride as inner satisfaction with a job well done, a job in which we feel our investment made a difference. Pride to me is in the realm of earned self-respect. Pride does not have to be boastful or arrogant or even spoken.

Recently, I attended an awards ceremony of RLG International, a company known for honoring its employees. "The Best of the Best" annual dinner recognizes the top accomplishments in the company; award recipients may include office staff as well as top-dollar and project producers. It was heartwarming to see the smiling family members of the employees sitting in the ballroom, watching their loved ones receive recognition for successes that they knew they, too, had played a part in. At my table, one of the employees leaned over to comment, "I must tell you how proud we are to be affiliated with such a fine company!"

Just for today, I will name silently the areas of my work in which I can take real pride. I may even share them with someone close to me.

"Gratitude is not only the greatest of virtues, but the parent of all others."

—Marcus Tullius Cicero

How and when do you experience gratitude in your day? I recall the first time I read the theologian Henri Nouwen. I had never thought that I prayed, but Nouwen spoke of prayer as gratitude, and then I realized I prayed often. I give thanks and express gratitude daily—for my health, loved ones, friends, and for work that fills me.

How do you express gratitude to those with whom you work? It need not be in fanciful words; a simple thank-you can mean a lot to another. Years ago I worked with a group of other clinicians, all of whom were very busy. During the day, I would stop at my mailbox to pick up telephone messages, and often, along with the pink message slips, I found brief thank-you notes. Such thoughtfulness always warmed my spirit; I knew I mattered to my co-workers.

Just for today, I will acknowledge that gratitude is a part of my spiritual growth. I will recognize that I don't move toward wholeness alone.

May 6 ～ *Graciousness*

"Deliberate with caution, but act with decision; and yield with graciousness. . . ."

—Charles Hole

Often people think of graciousness as "feminine." I like to think of graciousness as politeness and respect. When we work in an environment where people treat each other with civility, we feel more relaxed and work efficiently. It does not "cost" us any more to be gracious to one another. On the contrary, rudeness drains energy and decreases productivity in the workplace.

Some see graciousness as old-fashioned, yet I have seen many a work environment in which it is the norm. Although many people believe that the industry or profession we work in dictates the norms, this is not true—the leaders set the tone. While working with a group in a Detroit motor parts factory—an industry in which the workers are frequently stereotyped as being gruff and rude—I saw some of the most polite behaviors ever witnessed in a workplace.

Just for today, I will be gracious to others. In at least two kind actions, I will express kindness toward my co-workers.

"If you have lower than a 10 percent turnover, there is a problem. And if you have higher than say 20 percent, there is a problem."

—William Magovern

Retention issues loom large in today's workplace. On the one hand, the largest private employer in the United States currently is Manpower Temporaries. And on the other hand, employers are concerned about retaining good employees. I often wonder how high turnover rates affect the attitudes of employees. Poor retention is definitely costly—in dollars and in spirit; it feeds anxieties, blocking spiritual growth. Hiring and training a new employee is so expensive that many employers today are asking most of their employees what they need to stay.

Some firms are reviewing the structure of their workdays or the amount of travel they assign. Others are trying to learn why they have problems retaining women. Many companies hold off-site retreats to focus on team building. Some conduct exit interviews. One large health care facility offers a unique benefit: once a month, outside speakers come in to discuss a nonwork-related subject. Employees rank this high in their attitude surveys. Such mindfulness builds company loyalty and appreciation and strengthens employee retention. Employers are learning . . . from their employees.

Just for today, I will ask what holds me in my work and why I want to stay. I will question what role my spirit plays in my decision to stay or leave.

May 8 ⁓ *Assessment*

"I think self-awareness is probably the most important thing towards beginning as a champion."

—Billie Jean King

Can you remember the last time you underwent any kind of assessment? The way people react to assessments is shaped positively or negatively by their past experiences. Assessment means evaluation, to which most of us have a mixed response. Our fears can surely surface when we know we are being assessed.

Assessment tools can be extremely helpful in hiring people, developing people, and in identifying personality factors. However, people also like to use assessment tools to learn more about themselves. Recently, I used a leadership profile assessment with a business group. The group members had assessed one another—and themselves—on many aspects of their behavior, rating them on a five-point scale. As they read their summary score aloud to one another, I saw heads nodding in acknowledgment of where they and their peers needed to grow. This honest feedback became invaluable as they worked on restructuring their roles in the group. It also brought a level of self-awareness that could certainly aid in their spiritual growth.

Just for today, I will reflect on what assessments could be helpful to me. I will ask myself how open I am to assessing my progress on behavior changes.

"Know thyself. Nothing in excess. The Self is required to balance the Self."

—Ralph Blum

How often do you do a self-evaluation? And on what? Self-evaluation can certainly prepare us for any feedback to come, if it is honest.

A young colleague, Ellen, was a bit unsure about her meeting presentation skills as she prepared to begin work in a retreat setting. She was fearful and open about her fears. She questioned whether she would be credible and able to deliver. While giving her presentation, Ellen was also self-evaluating, asking herself, "I wonder how they think I am doing?" She actually stopped right in the midst of her talk and asked aloud, "How am I doing?" The entire room broke into laughter; the retreat participants found her earnestness and vulnerability so refreshing. She felt very relieved as they all affirmed her—"Just keep going; you're doing great!" How seldom we see that scene. So many times we walk away wondering, stuck with our own distorted criticisms, which can be dead wrong.

Just for today, I will do a self-evaluation in some aspect of my work life, knowing it will help me hold myself accountable and better prepare me for honest feedback.

May 10 ⁓ *Accountability*

"We are accountable only to ourselves for what happens to us in our lives."

—Mildred Newman

To whom are you accountable and for what? How do you hold yourself accountable? We all need to be held accountable and need others to help us with that. While most of us do not want someone checking our work or standing over us, we know there is a real need to be held accountable.

A good friend of mine had been active in the Twelve Step program of Alcoholics Anonymous (AA) for twenty-plus years and still loyally attended weekly meetings. One day another friend asked him why he still attended AA meetings even though he had such a good sobriety. "Why, that's easy," he exclaimed. "I need AA to hold me accountable. I cannot lie to my AA group." A client I was coaching once said something similar; he was a faithful journal writer, putting in daily entries. When asked about it, he said, "I could never lie to my journal; it holds me accountable."

Just for today, I will hold myself accountable. I will honor my obligations to others as well as to myself.

"If the people will lead, the leaders will follow."

—Robert Kelley

How much of your day is spent in following? How much in leading others? Most of us spend about 70 to 90 percent of our day following. The success of any organization is due to the work of 80 percent of the workers; the named leaders contribute about 20 percent. In speaking about followership, we are not talking about sheep following—doing what they are told—but rather about the interdependence that produces success. People who know what to do without being told—those who possess a strong sense of ethics and act with independence—exemplify followership. Team cultures often reflect followership principles.

When Cynthia, the CEO of a firm with thirteen thousand employees, decided to take a month off to be with her family, she did so with confidence. Through a team culture, she had developed good followership; she valued her employees. They knew when to lead and when to follow. How successful would *your* CEO, president, or director be without followership—without trusted people who make it all happen?

Just for today, I will focus on followership—how my work contributes to the whole in any project—and will acknowledge that my spirit needs to balance leading and following.

May 12 ～ *Self-Expression*

"It is only by expressing all that is inside that the purer streams come."

—Brenda Ueland

How would others describe your ability to express yourself? If we allow ourselves to express our own original thoughts at work, people are often receptive. We in turn feel we are a vital part of a work system.

Dan had been a long-term bank employee, rising from bank teller to vice president over his twenty-year career. Now he felt stuck; he wondered how he could feel alive again at work, having done most of the jobs there. Most of the situations he faced seemed repetitive, just variations on old themes. A single book on self-expression made a difference for Dan. After reading it, he had an "aha," or a "wake-up call." For years he had failed to express many of his ideas. Now, however, he realized that his work culture did value new ideas and feedback. Almost overnight, Dan began to share his thoughts about improving the system. Doing so made him feel alive, valued, and appreciated. We don't have to be at a vice-presidential level to focus on self-expression; it is our work right.

Just for today, I will assess how clearly and how often I express myself, understanding that self-expression helps me know myself better and lets others know me as well.

"Out beyond ideas of wrongdoing and rightdoing, there is a field. I'll meet you there."

—Rumi

What do you do when you disagree with others at work? Some years ago Maria, a very efficient secretary, was typing up my speech on healthy communication in the workplace. One of the lines was "I will disagree and say when I do." But Maria typed "I will disagree and *stay* when I do." When I saw that, I teasingly asked her if that was true for her. She blushed and laughed when she said, "Why, yes, that is indeed what I do, and I had good teachers in my Scandinavian family."

This story stuck like oatmeal. Too often people think that disagreement is a personal vote against them, rather than against a plan or idea. Some employees get defensive or attempt persuasion; others leave physically or psychologically. One useful tool is to simply state, "I understand how you see it; thanks for explaining." This statement "holds it out there," which not only shows respect for differences but also serves as a bridge to genuine dialogue. It can take us to the "field" that Rumi talks about.

Just for today, I will focus on listening carefully to others' perspectives, knowing that with an open heart, I can be open to accepting and respecting differing views.

May 14 ～ *Collaboration*

"Those who believe in dignity, meaning and community and who want to create the . . . best place to work, must somehow, someway involve everybody."

—Marvin R. Weisbord

How often do we hear the word *silos* when talking about work—meaning that groups are working in isolation and not collaboration.

When Sue first came to her company as president, she appreciated the healthy competition; it was a lively workplace. Over time, however, she discovered that the spirited competition had turned into cutthroat contentiousness. In an all-day company-wide meeting with an outside facilitator, she made certain that each work group was composed of employees from various levels and divisions. Toward the end of the day, she presented the company's newest and biggest client—the largest in their history—whose projects would require true collaboration. Announcing that "We are going to do things differently around here," Sue named team leaders and the collaboration began. This work required "thinking outside the box" for most of the groups. Some struggled and protested, but a cultural shift had started. With strong, well-liked leaders, the collaboration took hold and silos eventually tumbled down. Sue was impressed with the vitality of the groups; no silos were in sight.

Just for today, I will look for possibilities for collaboration, knowing that "the whole is always greater than the sum of its parts."

"Meaningful work is important; so is a decent salary. Finding ways to bridge those frequently divergent paths may be one of the key quests of our generation."

—Norman Boucher and Laura Tennen

What comes to mind when you think of balance? Too often people think of balance coming *after* work hours—in balancing family and work. Seldom addressed is how to incorporate balance *into* the workday so that we are not leaving work exhausted, bringing "leftovers" to our families, friends, and communities.

Balance is usually measured in time. A different perspective is to look at balance through energy expended—mentally, emotionally, and physically. Several people have told me they find balance by closing their office door for fifteen minutes—quiet time they use for meditation or reflection. Checkout clerks describe taking a brisk walk during their lunch breaks. Doing simple exercises at your desk or station is another way to stimulate your muscles and nervous system. Balancing our expended energy means we are able to leave work where it belongs and not be preoccupied with it during our free time. To know balance at work, we need to balance our energies emotionally, physically, and mentally. This is the balance our spirits seek.

Just for today, I will focus on balancing how I spend my energy emotionally, physically, and mentally. I will commit to tending a balanced spirit.

May 16 ⌒ *Aesthetics*

"The artistic mind looks beyond convention, stretching the expected to explore what can be."

—John Dalla Costa

What aesthetics in your workplace nurture you? How can you enhance your work environment aesthetically? Perhaps you play soft music or display a plant, a poster, or a meaningful object on your desk or at your workstation.

Aesthetics affect how we work. Subconsciously, they soothe our minds and nurture the spirit through the right hemisphere of the brain, the nonverbal creative hemisphere. An aesthetic object need not be large to feed the spirit. I often notice that taxicab drivers hang some form of art onto the dash or from the rearview mirror. Many people find that they respond not only to aesthetic objects but to the color of paint on their walls, to the color of their furniture, or to the texture of small carvings sitting on their desks. Can you identify an object in your surroundings that you feel a connection to?

Just for today, I will enhance the aesthetics of my work environment. If I am traveling, I shall bring a small pleasing object with me.

"In Greek consciousness, Chaos and Gaia were partners, two primordial powers engaged in a duet of opposition and resonance, creating everything we know."

—Meg Wheatley

What is your personal response to the word *chaos*? For years, we thought that *chaos* was a negative term, referring to disorder, disarray, and confusion. Today, when changes occur in our work world, we often resist them and the accompanying chaos. Yet we have a need for chaos. In living with chaos, we find the life source of our creative power.

Computer scientists recently discovered that the chaotic movements of a system actually have a shape and a pattern. When a work system is dislodged from its stable state, for example, it enters a period of unpredictability and swings between the two states. Just when the entire system should fall apart, a "strange attractor" appears that almost magnetically draws the system into a visible shape. Something new is created.

Chaos reflects infinite possibilities. As we learn to live with rates of exponential change, it is helpful to understand the importance of chaos: without it, we could not have meaningful change.

Just for today, I will embrace chaos and be aware that a new form is being born.

May 18 ∼ Culture

"Culture is both an intellectual phenomenon and a moral one."

—Raisa M. Gorbachev

How would you describe your work culture? How do you feel when you enter your company? Our workplace culture refers to the values and behaviors that new employees, encouraged by long-standing employees, automatically follow. It took business leaders some years to realize why so many attempted mergers and acquisitions did not succeed: more than half failed due to mismatched cultures.

The size of an organization is not a barrier to a healthy culture. Companies such as 3M are known for fostering an environment of fluidity and freedom as well as mutual encouragement. Thus, 3M does well not only with its bottom-line performance, but also with the way it treats its employees—the company cares about feelings. Optimism and openness prevail at 3M.

Rod became very dissatisfied with his high-performing company. He found that the outward appearance of success was incongruent with the internal culture of disrespect, arrogance, and intimidation. Feelings were not valued and his attempts to change the culture were rejected. Rod knew he had much to offer a healthy culture; he decided to leave.

Just for today, I will be aware of how the culture at my workplace affects me. I will do my best to contribute to a positive and uplifting culture.

"Difficulties are meant to rouse, not discourage. The human spirit is to grow strong by conflict."

—William Ellery Channing

How is conflict handled in your work environment? Is it buried or unexpressed? Does it fill the air with tension? Or, is managing conflict honored in your workplace? Conflict is natural; it is what we do with it that, negatively or positively, affects our work environment.

When I encountered a small work group that clearly knew how to express conflict effectively, I asked, "Do you realize what you have here? This is so rare!" At that point, my client remarked with a smile, "We know it's natural; it's just not normal." How true. We typically accept the rules of our work culture. If that means formal politeness with conflict buried, we usually step into line. But eventually, this behavior becomes gossip and political "games." Yet burying feelings of conflict can lead to depression; whole companies could sometimes be diagnosed as "depressed." When conflict is managed effectively, however, productivity and creativity can increase. But perhaps most important, employees can enjoy their workplace and learn more about themselves and others through conflict.

Just for today, I will ask myself how I respond to conflict and whether I express conflict appropriately in my workplace.

"A business that makes nothing but money is a poor kind of business."

—Henry Ford

Have you ever had to work with diminished resources? In our public school systems, we find a glaring example of employees dealing with diminished resources. Teachers often buy standard supplies with their own money; this occurs in large metropolitan areas and lower-income states. One impressive story of overcoming such obstacles comes from Santa Fe, New Mexico—an area where teachers' salaries and educational ratings fall at the lowest end of the national rankings.

Realizing that schools in Santa Fe, a town known for its art, had limited art supplies, a group of residents decided to take action. They asked local restaurants and galleries to donate time and resources for a fund-raising event. The group then sold twenty-dollar tickets for an evening of "Edible Art"—gallery hopping and "grazing" on artistically prepared food. The tour has become an annual event in Santa Fe; everyone enjoys themselves, and the children have their art supplies. The group in Santa Fe found a unique solution to their school's problem; we, too, can work toward answering the call for help in our communities. Diminished resources can be the springboard for spirited creativity.

Just for today, I will review my resources—some may be tangible and others may be intangible. I will ask what is missing in my, or someone else's, life.

"Life shrinks or expands in proportion to one's courage."

—Anaïs Nin

What acts of courage do you see in your workplace? Is it truth telling? Is it expressing an original idea? Or, is it taking a stand for personal beliefs, even though it means breaking the rules of the organization?

Steve, the vice president of sales for a large equipment manufacturing firm, obtained his company's largest contract ever—for a buyer in China. The downside was that young children would be working in the Chinese manufacturing plant. When Steve handed the contract to his president and explained the downside, the president thrust it back into his hands and said, "You decide." Steve paused for a moment and then tore up the contract. No need for words; they made a moral decision.

While this is a dramatic example, we all know people who have taken courageous stands in their workplaces. We may have done it ourselves. When such challenges confront us, we can take a risk and be courageous. In doing so, we create a culture of honesty and integrity.

Just for today, I will reflect on my own challenges and ask myself what the next step might be.

May 22 ⌒ *Personal-Work Balance*

"Ultimately, the consequences of individuals' choices regarding work and family will depend, to a degree, on the overall organizational climate."

—Peter Senge

How do you balance your personal and work lives? Do you live your values by walking your talk?

I recall working with a young man named Josh who was ambitious and "on the way up." He had strived hard to get to his high position in his firm, a position that required considerable travel each week. He felt good about the "quality time" he allotted to spend with his wife and daughter when he was home for a few days at a time. Yet one day he sought help, tears rolling slowly down his face. He told a story about his six-year-old daughter, who had been asked to draw a picture of her family. When he came home, the picture was on the refrigerator. The drawing was of her mother and herself; her daddy was not in it.

Josh recognized that what he called work-family balance was merely a lie he told himself so he could justify his climb to financial success and his long work hours. His "balance" was a myth; he had been dishonest with himself and with his family. Josh faced a spiritual crisis honestly.

Just for today, I will seriously contemplate whether I keep balance in my life. What spirit-nurturing activities do I engage in and how often?

Insecurity ⌒ May 23

"Insecurity breeds treachery: If you are kind to people that hate themselves, they will hate you as well."

—Florence King

Do you know where, when, and with whom you feel insecure? It is important to know what threatens our feeling of competence. Sometimes it may be a "ghost" from the past—someone in our workday world who reminds us of a person we were uncomfortable around as a child. Perhaps a co-worker reminds us of our intimidating Uncle Lou or our mean-spirited older brother. It is natural to feel insecure at times, but when it's more than occasional, we need to do some inner work.

Maria was a very competent person yet felt insecure while presenting ideas to her work team. Maria had grown up in a highly critical family that was very stingy with positive feedback. Even though Maria had been a star student, her self-doubt remained firmly in place. At a friend's suggestion, she enrolled in a class called "Acting for Non-Actors." During the eight-week class, as she became more comfortable with herself, she broke through her self-consciousness and was even able to laugh at how fearful she'd been. By the time the class ended, she felt confident and transferred her newfound security to her workplace.

Just for today, I will do a "security inventory" and ask myself where and with whom I feel insecure. Then I'll take action to learn more about myself and my history.

May 24 ～ Exuberance

"You can employ men and hire hands to work for you, but you must win their hearts to have them work with you."

—Riori

When was the last time you felt exuberance, or extreme enthusiasm? People who influence us are usually those with such enthusiasm that we find it difficult not to follow. Obviously, the enthusiasm has to be sincere; we know when it is a "carnival barker" approach. Identify any models for exuberance in your work world. What are their traits? How do they inspire you?

Most people who are enthusiastic believe deeply in something. Successful work groups generally have at least one person who leads the energy, who is the voice of enthusiasm. Our energy can move other people and touch the part of them that wants to believe in possibilities. Without the belief in possibilities, we limit our progress. Exuberance is often what breaks down old paradigms.

Just for today, let me observe the exuberance in my life. How does enthusiasm affect my spirit?

Time ⌒ May 25

"Dwell as near as possible to the channel in which your life flows."

—Henry David Thoreau

What comes to mind when you think about time? Is it a quantity that you measure? Time is certainly how we measure our lives—in hours, years, or decades. We kill it, we waste it, we pass it, and we sometimes savor it. At work, it's easy to become clock-bound.

In the book *Timeshifting,* Stephan Rechtschaffen, M.D., of the Omega Institute explains the difference between mental time and emotional time. With mental time, concepts and thoughts come quickly, and we learn to rely on this. We stay "in our heads" and think rapidly. But when we think about emotional time, we are entering another realm. Emotional time is connected with the limbic system of the brain and has to do with our emotions, which we often run from. Emotional time demands that we slow down and breathe so feelings can have the time they need to surface. When we are using only mental time, we are imbalanced, limiting our creativity and crowding our spirits.

How can we join our emotional time with our mental time?

Just for today, I will focus on my breathing and concentrate on blending my emotional time with my mental time.

May 26 ⌒ *Perspective*

"Distance has the same effect on the mind as on the eye."

—Samuel Johnson

How often have you wondered about someone else's perspective? And how often have you judged a situation poorly or even mistakenly because of a different perspective? If most of us heard one another's perspectives, we could more fully understand each other's views and opinions.

A group was working on creating a new structure for their division. These six individuals had worked together for years and were a cohesive group. Yet as the meeting started, there was some tension in the air—"Whose idea would be the chosen one?" To lessen the tension, they agreed to take an unusual approach: The group members used a flip chart and presented their varying perspectives on why and how they thought the division should be restructured. They used color markers and symbols as well as words. After listening to each other's perspectives, the group had a deeper understanding of everyone's views. They were then able to find the similar threads and weave a new design for their division.

Just for today, I will pay attention to the opinions of others. When on the verge of judging, I will consider perspective.

"Learning how to learn is life's most important skill."

—Tony Buzan

Do you know your learning style? Have you ever felt inadequate as you watched someone else pick up a language quickly or play a musical instrument with little effort while you struggled? Often we forget that people have different learning styles. Yet, how we learn makes a keen difference in how we work.

Some years ago, Howard Gardner, a professor at Harvard, studied how people learn and found that there are seven "kinds of smart." The learning styles Gardner identified are verbal/linguistic, interpersonal, bodily/kinesthetic, musical/rhythmic, visual/spatial, logical/mathematical, and intrapersonal. He realized that all too often, we focus solely on verbal/linguistic intelligence and disregard the other six styles of learning.

With the increasing diversity in our workplaces today, it seems only natural that we would consider how different learning styles affect our work. Most people are not verbal/linguistic learners; we need to recognize this as we communicate in our work worlds. Being respectful of the multiple intelligences can only enhance self-esteem and improve our work productivity and creativity.

Just for today, I will ask myself how I feel most comfortable in learning. I will also attempt to discern and respect the learning styles of others.

May 28 ～ *Arrogance*

"There was one who thought he was above me, and he was above me until he had that thought."

—Elbert Hubbard

Being with an arrogant person can be intimidating—and harmful in the workplace. Arrogance surfaces in two different ways: First, we see arrogance as a cover for insecurity and inadequacy and a flight from feelings. Second, we see arrogance in people who have not yet had a spiritual awakening. Life has not yet given them a "wake-up call"—a call to consciousness—and they believe they are truly in charge of their worlds.

Consultant and author Harry Levinson says that many CEOs have traits of arrogance and narcissism. They tend to blame others or use rationalizations for their own failures and mistakes. One day, an executive vice president addressed his entire division. Afterward, I praised him on how genuine he was—and on how differently he came across from the man I had met two years earlier. "Well," he smiled, "you told me I had to do something about my arrogance and intimidation, and I did! Well, actually with a little help from my prostate cancer diagnosis . . . and I now feel more alive than ever."

Just for today, I will be watchful of any arrogance that creeps into me and attempts to hijack my spirit. I will ask myself what feeling might be driving my arrogance.

"Comparisons are odious."

—Fourteenth-century saying

Do you ever find yourself comparing yourself with another? Often when we are feeling insecure or inadequate, the comparisons commence. This of course is a put-down to ourselves. Comparing ourselves with others when we are feeling vulnerable can cause us to feel lesser-than. There are always those who are (fill in the blank)—smarter, more competent in some area, thinner, taller, younger, more popular.

If we must compare, we can do it in a positive way. We can identify role models for a behavior or trait we want to emulate. We can observe the modeled behavior and say, "That is how I want to be in that particular trait." Carrying images of those we highly respect, our heroes, helps us as we seek spiritual growth. We can choose not to compare negatively.

Just for today, I will ask myself whether I am comparing myself to someone else and whether it is for learning or for putting myself down.

May 30 〜 *Service*

"I don't know what your destiny will be, but one thing I know: the only ones among you who will be really happy are those who will have sought and found how to serve."

—Albert Schweitzer

Do you think of service when you think of work? Some people work in human service organizations, so service is part of their work. Many other organizations are not in human services yet still focus on serving.

Billy Weisman, the president of Weisman Enterprises in Minneapolis, believes in employees giving back to the communities that have shaped and supported them. As Weisman acts on his belief, his workforce is exposed to the needs in the community through a variety of volunteer activities. Employees are given work time to serve the community. They also volunteer for events that are held on weekends—the Race for the Cure for Mother's Day, the Special Olympics, or the Juvenile Diabetes JDF Walk. Volunteer projects include sponsoring classes in inner-city schools and feeding needy families through local organizations. One employee summed up the service work quite well: "It makes you feel really good inside and helps you realize that what you have is precious—and not to take things for granted."

Just for today, I will look at where I serve. I will explore how service can be incorporated more fully into my workplace, and I will take action.

Trust ⌒ May 31

"Trust is our trail guide through the wilderness of change."

—Bill McCarthy

For our spirits to grow, we need to be in a trusting environment. Trust is the reliance on the nonverbal communication of another in a high-risk situation. Aware that a hospital staff had very low trust, we took the group out for two days of rock climbing. There they had to belay one another, that is, hold the "lifeline" climbing rope in their hands while anchored to trees and boulders. They had to literally put their lives in one another's hands. When they chose belayers, mistrust surfaced immediately. The negotiations were tense; one woman refused another, saying she did not trust herself. Another cried as she blurted out, "No way, I don't trust you!" Afterwards, in the group meeting, they all shared their vulnerable feelings and their excitement in having learned so much so quickly. They eagerly translated their experiences into their work; rather than the cold edge of mistrust, warmth and vulnerability filled the group. The group members were able to transfer this back into their work setting with renewed spirits.

Just for today, I will ask myself how high my trust is in myself, in my co-workers, and in my close relationships.

June

Differences ∽ June 1

"Differences challenge assumptions."

—Anne Wilson Schaef

What kind of differences do you face at work? While cultural differences in ethnicity, race, and gender are obvious, differences in our principles and values are harder to detect. Yet these differences are more likely to become areas of concern. Working through differences can push our values.

Recently when a group of Tibetan Americans working in a major hospital learned that His Holiness the Dalai Lama would be lecturing in their city, they all asked for the same day off. The hospital had been very pleased with the Tibetans' work ethic and so wanted to cooperate. Yet at first the hospital didn't understand just how important this lecture was to the Tibetans in exile; they were willing to give up their jobs rather than miss seeing His Holiness. This value difference was one that hospital administrators were not prepared for, but because the Tibetans approached their managers with unwavering dignity and respect, the managers agreed to outsource their work for that day.

Just for today, let me understand the principles underlying our differences and honor those differences wherever possible.

June 2 ～ Quality

"Quality is never an accident; it is always the result of high intention, sincere effort, intelligent direction, and skillful execution; it represents the wise choice of many alternatives."

—William A. Foster

How would others describe the quality of your work? And how would you describe it? Do you take pride in the work you do? What happens when you know you did not give your all?

Recently the president of Delta Dental spoke at a meeting I attended. He reported that his employees felt so strongly about the quality of their work that they guaranteed 100 percent refunds if they did not meet their deadline in paying customer claims. What stood out strongly in his presentation was not the list of ten guarantees, but the fact that the entire company was committed to such quality standards. This was the result of team building. The employees committed to carrying these quality standards not because they were paid incredibly high wages but rather because they and the company's officers shared the value of quality.

Just for today, I will focus on the quality of my work and ask myself whether I am meeting my own standards.

"So much of what we call management consists of making it difficult for people to work."

—Peter F. Drucker

Have you ever sensed that someone was attempting to micromanage your work?

Tom was recently named general manager at an electrical parts manufacturing plant. The president had asked him to take responsibility for generating new business as well as for managing eight plant managers. Tom micromanaged the plants, which fostered resentment and left little time for working on new business development. The plant managers were upset and felt they were not trusted; yet they kept quiet because they believed the president would not take their concern seriously.

In an all-division communications seminar, the seminar leader introduced the issue of micromanagement. When she saw heads nodding, she pursued the issue; the managers finally spoke up. Tom heard some difficult feedback, but it came just in time. The president had been concerned with Tom's lack of time for new business development. With this issue out in the open, Tom could admit how overwhelmed he had felt with his new role, and he began letting go of his controlling behaviors.

Just for today, I will ask myself when and how I might be micromanaging and how I can help anyone else with this issue.

June 4 ⌖ *Injustice*

"The best way of avenging thyself is not to become like the wrongdoer."

—Marcus Aurelius

Have you witnessed injustices in your workplace? Jud, a high-profile outsider, was hired to lead a large department in a health care company. Nancy, the competent employee who had organized the start-up of this department years ago, was satisfied with her job and welcomed the new department head; they got along quite well.

Within six months after Jud's arrival, the company marked its fortieth anniversary with a week-long celebration. Jud was asked to address the health care specialists at the awards banquet. He recognized only the employees he had brought on board and ignored the department's history, including the contributions of Nancy and her colleagues. Nancy did not seem surprised; she had felt other injustices all along. Nancy's colleagues all reached out to her; she felt their loyalty.

Nancy did nothing about this, but life had its natural consequences. Within the following six months, Jud was released.

Just for today, I will explore how I might be a part of injustices in my work. I will focus on taking appropriate stands whenever possible and accept that it's sometimes wiser to let life take its course.

"The power to question is the basis of all human progress."

—Indira Gandhi

How and what do you question at work? Questioning can take many forms. For example, we may ask pragmatic, sensible questions of the more creative, experienced, or knowledgeable people in our work group. "How will we implement this? Has it been tried elsewhere?" Such questions help the whole of any work group. Another form of questioning, however, can throw people off, create doubt, and slow down the entire work group.

Janice asked questions that had a competitive edge to them, which often triggered irritation. Her questioning was manipulative and not for the good of the whole. She asked questions such as, "Have you considered that this might not be the best approach to solving this problem?" rather than stating her disagreement directly. Sometimes a person who observes this game playing can make a polite inquiry or a comment on the group process. This can often stop the manipulative behavior.

Just for today, I will pay attention to my own questions. Are they truly to seek information or are they "see me" questions?

June 6 ～ Victims

"Never be bullied into silence. Never allow yourself to be made a victim. Accept no one's definition of your life; define yourself."

—Harvey Feinstein

Have you ever noticed the power of the workplace "victim"? These are the people for whom nothing is ever enough. Often they have long lists of unexpressed wants or demands. Yet they are not assertive; no one else knows what is wanted. All the colleagues know is that somehow they have failed this person.

Michael held his work group hostage through his humble victim style. Many of his co-workers felt sorry for him and became loyal advocates, but Michael would never raise his issues in meetings. Over time, the group began to notice how much energy he drained from them. His very presence suggested that somehow they owed him something. Eventually Michael's boss confronted his limited skills in getting his needs met and asked him to change or leave. Michael finally looked at his self-sabotaging behavior and made changes to keep his job. He found it helpful to read books on victimization, which taught him how to connect his learned role with his family history.

Just for today, I will acknowledge the power of the "victim." I will gently remind myself that if I am feeling sorry for myself, it is up to me to bring my issues to the table.

"The foundations of a person are not in matter but in spirit."

—Ralph Waldo Emerson

How do you tend your spirit at work? Do you display any pieces of art or of nature in your office to remind you of your spirituality? Our spirits require attention; symbols can often serve as personal reminders that our spirit is ever present.

One colleague reads a poetry passage before starting his workday. Another friend has a rock on her desk that symbolizes her spirit—a reminder of the spirit in all matter. One office group had a high number attending Twelve Step groups—AA, Al-Anon, and ACOA (Adult Children of Alcoholics)—both over lunch hours and after work. They recognized that to live their programs they needed to follow the program principles at work. One way they did this was by placing a box marked "God's Box" in an office file cabinet. During the day, as people needed to release what they could not control, they would write the issue down on paper and put it in the box. It did not take long for others in the company to start using the box too.

Just for today, I will recognize the importance of paying attention to my spirit at work and know that my spirit needs tending, even (or especially) at work.

June 8 ～ *Authenticity*

"May the inward and outward be as one."

—Socrates

The word *authentic* means being faithful to the original, being real and not false. When we're authentic, we're also true to our own spirits or character.

At a national business conference, I heard a speaker discuss authenticity in the workplace. Her manner was very contained, and during her presentation she moved deliberately from slide to slide. At the end of her address, she spoke about progress—financial progress. Many in the audience were disappointed because the speaker, to them, did not seem authentic. They connected authenticity with being warm and gregarious and having principles higher than money.

The speaker not did appear to be authentic to many, yet she was true to herself. Unfortunately, we often ignore the fact that authenticity means just that—being true to ourselves. At work, we must remember that we are all individuals and that our attempts at being true to our own spirits and character will likely differ from how our co-workers work at being authentic.

Just for today, I will appreciate the different expressions of authenticity and will not judge how others express themselves.

"The curious paradox is that when I accept myself just as I am, then I can change."

—Carl Rogers

Have you ever become obsessed with something going on at work? Or worse, have you ever had to listen to a friend, mate, or colleague obsess about a work situation? Obsession truly hijacks the spirit: it crowds out rational thought and honest feelings. Usually, we obsess because we cannot control someone else. Ironically, obsession usually renders us powerless.

When Hank became jealously obsessed about a co-worker on a project (also the manager's favorite), he did not see how he was giving away his power to his co-worker. Yet his co-worker's behavior was actually in charge of Hank's brain—Hank no longer controlled his own thoughts and feelings. The very thought of his co-worker took him directly away from his work. Hank's obsession probably consumed about 40 percent of his work-time energy; at home it stole hours of his sleep. Finally, Hank saw his employee assistance provider (EAP) and together they developed a plan to help Hank let go of his obsession; the plan included meditation and journaling his thoughts and feelings. In time, Hank regained control of his life and his power.

Just for today, I will consider what I hold on to for too long. I will take time to meditate and clear my head of all thoughts. In doing so, I will feel my inner power.

June 10 ⌒ *Problem Solving*

"The significant problems we face cannot be solved at the same level of thinking we were at when we created them."

—Albert Einstein

How do you approach problem solving? Too often we attempt a quick fix rather than taking the time to reflect on the problem's history. One financial services firm requires every new employee to take a problem-solving test, recognizing that it, like any other business, does and will have problems.

Recently, a group of executives had a heated discussion about sales figures. Sales were down, but why? The competition was doing well, while this company had just lost another big client. With the help of an outside consultant, the group backed up and learned the principles of problem solving. The executives realized they could not go forward until they went back to analyze the problem. Although the group members had strong entrepreneurial skills, they lacked a model for effective problem solving. Once they learned how to search for relevant data and analyze information, they could identify and prioritize their options. With these new skills in hand, they had renewed excitement; now they understood their mistakes and developed a forward-reaching plan.

Just for today, I will examine how I solve problems and where I might need some skill development to better face my challenges.

"To love what you do and feel that it matters—how could anything be more fun?"

—Katherine Graham

Most of us spend the greatest number of our waking hours at work. Our work gives our lives meaning; it is a source of our self-esteem, our values, our quality of life, and often our social network. Unfortunately, many people equate status at work with titles and economics, rather than recognizing a position as contributing to the "sum of the parts" that makes the whole. All work is important, and all workers deserve to be treated with dignity. Imagine if the mailroom personnel walked out or the sanitary engineers went on strike.

I recall an elderly Greek man who tended all the outdoor plants at the office building where I once worked. He took great pride in his work; he even talked to the flowers as he worked. When he turned one hundred years old, the building's managers decided to honor him with a party to celebrate not just his years but also his work. Almost all the tenants in the building attended; they all recognized how greatly this man's work mattered to him and how his work benefited others as well.

Just for today, let my actions demonstrate that my work matters to me. I will recognize that my duties, no matter how seemingly insignificant, contribute to my company's success.

June 12 ～ *Changing*

"Fluidity and discontinuity are central to the reality in which we live."

—Mary Catherine Bateson

Our childhood photos are testaments of our physical changes and growth. Unfortunately, we don't have such a barometer to see how the systems around us, or how we ourselves, are changing. Eventually history will tell us.

How readily we accept change and how willing we are to make change is critical in today's world of technological advancement. Yet with so many changes, it is more important than ever to be able to stay true to ourselves. This often requires a period of reflection. When we do decide to make changes in how we are at work, we must be willing to practice. First, we must make the commitment to change and then work in incremental steps to achieve that change.

When Harvey learned he had to make serious changes in his demeanor toward his co-workers and customers, he felt overwhelmed by the long list of things he had to work on. Yet he began and in time, he learned that his greatest fear—that people wouldn't let go of their old pictures of him—did not occur. Instead, they gave him positive feedback.

Just for today, I will ask myself how I see myself changing and will continue to practice new behaviors.

"What is this self-inflicted wound by shooting myself in the foot?"

—Anonymous

Have you ever found yourself "shooting yourself in the foot" through self-sabotaging behaviors?

Laura had no idea how she was contributing to her own downfall. When Laura was hired from outside the organization, she immediately gained a high-status title yet felt insecure since she had relatively little experience in the industry. Early on, she learned through the senior management that both clients and employees saw her as condescending and arrogant. Feeling "caught," Laura decided to connect with her subordinates in order to block negative feedback. She gossiped to the employees, revealing information that had been shared with her in confidence. When an outside consultant began working with the group on its dysfunctional communication and lack of "team," the stories tumbled out. Laura's divisive behaviors not only had been self-sabotaging, but had sabotaged the entire team as well. With the consultant's support, Laura faced her behaviors and recognized that she needed to be honest about her feelings of inadequacy and self-doubt.

Just for today, I will ask myself what my own self-sabotaging behaviors have been and take the first step toward changing them. I will ask trusted others for feedback, if necessary.

June 14 ～ *Cultural Differences*

"They condemn what they do not understand."

—Marcus Tullius Cicero

How do you view differences at work? Walking through your workplace, you may detect a number of differences in employees—ethnic origins, skin color, gender, dress, work styles, religious customs, or dialect. Often we see two major biases operating regarding differences. Some people think, "We are all the same. I see no differences." Others believe, "We are so different that we cannot possibly come together on planning and goals." Neither of these biases serves an organization well.

Eric had made many judgments about the new employees from other ethnic groups. He saw how "oddly" they dressed, how differently they handled time, and how infrequently they expressed their feelings. Eric saw differences as negative. Then he attended a seminar on cultural diversity, in which the participants talked about their countries of origins. Upon hearing these stories, Eric was surprised to learn how distanced he had become from the immigration stories of his own ancestors. He humbly reminded himself that, perhaps with the exception of Native Americans, we in the United States all are or descend from immigrants.

Just for today, I will remember my roots and be grateful for the gifts I have received from my own country of origin.

"The only time we're aware of the 'I' (eye) is when there's something wrong with it."

—Huston Smith

How cunning the ego! Have you ever found yourself seduced by your ego's needs?

Our egos lie to us, telling us how important we are with our "stickers" of status, title, and high-profile friends. Our egos are a central source of our self-esteem but are destructive if we gullibly believe them.

When Sherry was called into a meeting with her firm's partners, she assumed it was to receive praise and glory for all her accomplishments. When she entered the room, however, she was embarrassed and shocked to find clients sitting among the partners. She thought of leaving. However, trusting those in the room, she stayed to hear their feedback. In a caring confrontation, the group members voiced their concerns about how her ego seemed to be taking her away from her core self and harming her relationships with all those present. Although Sherry was in tears, she felt a deep relief come over her. Within months, she was back on her path, grateful that people cared enough to let her know the dangers of the ego.

Just for today, I will imagine myself stripped of all status and possessions and feel the strength of what remains—my inner power, my spirit.

June 16 ～ *Leading Authentically*

"It is high time that we had lights that are not incendiary torches."

—George Sand

What does authentic leadership look like? Recently, in a company's leadership seminar, I asked a work group to describe the attributes of authentic leadership. They came up with positive traits, such as honesty, humility, empathy, and consideration. Suddenly one person said, "I don't get it; why are you making *authentic* sound like something so one sided? It can also be ruthless, greedy, and dominating—what about Hitler?" With this, we discussed the fact that many of us defined authentic in only positive, idealized terms. Later, a guest spoke on authentic leadership. Some of the group were upset when they heard him talking extensively about his employees and financial goals—all were number goals. Others were quick to jump in, reminding the group that he did come across as an authentic leader. Like some other leaders, he had shades of self-centeredness and domination. We were reminded that just because someone does not meet our views of an idealized self does not mean he or she is inauthentic. Authentic means being real!

Just for today, I will contemplate whether my leaders are being their true selves.

"Genuine power is power with—pseudo power, power over."

—M. P. Follett

What comes to mind when you think about power? Do you see power in negative terms, or as an expression of one's ability and inner strength?

All too often we use the word *power* to connote negative meanings. We may hear others say, "She is power hungry!" or "He is really into power!" When we hear such phrases, we usually visualize someone who is domineering, ruthless, and probably arrogant. With these images in mind, many of us deny our power—our ability to influence others. We need not shy away from our power; we can learn to use power responsibly and for the greater good.

Rachel, a new college faculty member, never felt powerful as a senior professor. She was overwhelmed with work and felt she had no control over her students, much like parents often feel with their children. Rachel was a friendly and outgoing person, but she decided that she also needed to become more firm. Rachel's students were surprised to learn that her warmth did not mean she would lower her academic standards. When Rachel faced her power, she learned that she had feared losing herself by accepting her power as a senior professor. Once she was able to use power in a style that was comfortable to her, she became a much better professor.

Just for today, I will accept my real sense of power and identify the impact I have on others throughout my workday.

June 18 ～ *Determination*

"Diamonds are only chunks of coal, that stuck to their jobs, you see."

—Malcolm Forbes

How has your determination paid off for you in your life? So often it is difficult to know when to continue pushing forward and when to let go of a project or an idea.

Leslie wanted to change the culture of her small company. She realized that achieving her goals would require determination. Yet determination was not enough; she knew that she also needed a well-developed plan for the changes to stick in her industry of computer systems, an industry that was rapidly changing. She carefully laid out a detailed plan to achieve her goals, including all incremental steps, with quarterly reviews. She knew real change would take at least five years. At times along the way, Leslie became self-doubting; her determination waned. At times, it seemed that the company was moving backward. Each year, however, Leslie met with her management team and together they assessed the progress of the program. Indeed, the program progressed as planned.

Just for today, I will ask myself what results my determination has produced in my life and accept that some things take time.

"It is through creating, not possessing, that life is revealed."

—Vida D. Scudder

How do you experience creativity in your work life? Is it through sharing your knowledge with co-workers? Or is it in designing new methods for routine tasks?

Mike was the head of an organization that truly wanted to change how people behaved in the work-place. He brought in a consulting group that specialized in human development skills. Willing to make mistakes, Mike undertook the project to create interpersonal skill training for all of the company's ten thousand employees. Many employees were initially reluctant to participate in this new initiative.

One day the work group tried out some of the new exercises they had developed to expand creative problem-solving skills. They did one-minute consultations with one another on work problems, moving around the room from one person to the next. By the end of the exercise, the group members were delighted with their own creative ideas, as well as with their ability to so efficiently help one another. A renewed spirit of creativity began to spring forth throughout the company.

Just for today, I will appreciate my creativity and make room for it to appear in my work.

June 20 ～ *Doing Good*

"When I do good, I feel good."

—Randy Way

This quote says it plain and simple. Can you think of a time when you "did good" and could claim that to yourself? Usually we do best at what we are good at, so if we want to feel good, we need to focus on our strengths. At work, however, some of us do not claim our good work or are extremely modest about our achievements. We may have difficulty acknowledging or accepting what we do well.

We all have innate gifts that allow us to do "good" for others through our work. Good work surely does not have to be in the nature of the work, like a social service agency. We can "do good" at work by being courteous to others, recognizing what we are good at, and accepting the credit where and when it is due. Doing so strengthens our spirits.

Just for today, I will ask myself where I am doing good at work and allow the accompanying good feelings to surface.

"Of nature is independence a reality."

—Ruth Nanden Anshen

Is cooperation evident in your workplace? Because cooperative efforts are not always visible at work, I sometimes use an experiential exercise to demonstrate the power of cooperation and how it can shape our work environment. Recently, when consulting with a work group, I asked employees to split into groups of ten to a tarp. The groups were then informed that the tarps represented sinking ships and that their charge was to overturn, or "right," the ships (turn the tarps over) so they did not drown. They were given twelve minutes to right their ships.

Some groups analyzed the situation first; other groups jumped to ends of the tarps. During the exercise, the group members shared ideas, experimented, and rotated leadership. At the end, each group described what it took to reach the goal. Success was always achieved through full cooperation of the team and through creative problem solving. Beyond that, the most successful group (which righted their ship in three minutes) created a competitive and cooperative spirit that came from working together.

Just for today, I will focus on how I cooperate with others. How do I share my knowledge? How do I feel in the spirit of cooperation?

June 22 ⌒ *The Invisible*

"The unseen design of things is more harmonious than the seen."

—Heraclitus

To trust the invisible means trusting what the spirit can bring. We also must know that, as writer Rene Daumal says, "The door to the invisible can only be opened through that which is visible." It is up to us, in the material world, to open that door. As we learn to trust the invisible and how it helps shape our daily lives—*including* our work lives—we can let go more readily and accept what comes to us.

Ellen, age fifty-two, faced a new life. In a new town, where she had recently earned a management degree, she set out to start a consulting service. Ellen saw a long, hard path ahead of her; she began to wonder, "Am I too old? Am I not competent?" Despite her insecurity, Ellen began moving down her path by focusing on two areas: She made new contacts each day, and she asked for help by praying and talking with, in her words, her Higher Power. For more than a year, she seemed to be on a roller coaster, yet she did not miss a day of talking with the invisible. Today, she has a thriving consulting business.

Just for today, I will tune in to the "invisible" by listening with more than my ears. I will know that my "seventh sense" is ever present.

"We teach others how to treat us."

—Anonymous

Do you treat yourself as well as you treat others? Jim, a fourteen-year employee, had his sights on becoming a plant manager at his company. He had been a valued assistant for many years and had treated all his employees well. The last time the owners talked about hiring a new plant manager, they had suggested to Jim that he would get the position. But then they hired an outsider for the job—without informing Jim. Jim's work group was furious, but Jim hid his own feelings. A few months later, another plant manager position opened up. Jim became excited again, especially after the owners' glowing praise in his annual review, but again they chose someone else.

Jim spent long hours talking with friends and his wife about the situation. Finally, Jim put his shame aside and confronted the two owners. He sat tall and painfully told them what he had experienced; he made it clear that he could no longer accept this kind of treatment. The owners listened attentively and apologized sincerely. Within four months, Jim became a plant manager.

Just for today, I will treat myself with the same respect I give others. By doing so, I will teach others how to treat me.

June 24 ⁓ *Being in the Present*

"It is not the things we accomplish that are important, it is the very act of living that is truly important."

—Dr. Bill Jackson

Have you ever wondered how many hours of your day are spent "being here now"—staying in the present? How much time do you spend reviewing the past or thinking ahead? How does it feel when you are meeting with others and they are not totally with you? Most people feel hurt and irritated when they know they are not being truly heard. But have you ever thought about how often you might have treated other people like nonpersons as you hurried to get on with your work?

In reviewing behaviors of outstanding leaders, I have observed that many are able to stand fully present when talking with someone. They are "here now," giving their undivided attention. Jack, who was in a rush, was attempting to give his boss, Sally, a message about a meeting. Sally, standing with a small group, focused her attention fully on the person speaking to her. Jack's furtive glances, foot shuffling, and stares could not detract Sally from her conversation. Jack later said, "I think I learned what it means to be in the present, and I think I know why Sally is such a respected leader."

Just for today, I will practice being in the present and see how it affects my workday and my relationships with others.

"Those who give too much attention to trifling things become generally incapable of great things."

—François de La Rochefoucauld

Most of us know when we are focused. We are fully present and totally absorbed in our work at hand; we have no sense of time. Sometimes we hear people refer to "being in it." It's important to know what we need in order to focus. Some of us need total quiet; others need a clean work space.

Jeb said that he was having trouble focusing on writing summaries of his accounting assessments. In Jeb's annual review, his manager asked him if there were problems at home. Surprised, Jeb said, "Why, no. I just have a hard time with all the distractions around me." Together they came up with a simple solution. Jeb moved his furniture so he could face inward, and his concentration immediately improved. He also made an important discovery. When he stayed focused on his work, he stayed with himself and was more fully in touch with his feelings as well as his thoughts.

Just for today, I will pay attention to what I need to stay focused.

June 26 ~ *Life Planning*

"What do you plan to do with your one wild and precious life?"

—Mary Oliver

What do your life plans look like? How does your work life fit in with your life plan? Our work is not an entity separate from our lives; it is intentionally, or unintentionally, a part of our overall life plan.

Craig had worked in the financial industry for more than twenty-five years. He enjoyed his work and in everyone's eyes was a success. At age fifty-five, he was considering moving to a large city to take an executive position in his firm. During this same period, however, he and his wife began working with a life-planning consultant. As they identified their goals, Craig now faced a real dilemma: accepting this new position would delay their plans for world travel by at least five years. Financially secure, Craig did not have to take the position. After long, intimate discussions, he and his wife decided they did not need the move, the status, or the money associated with the new job; they chose to live their life plan and to begin their world travel. Craig has no regrets.

Just for today, I will focus on how my life's work is contributing to my life planning. I will ask myself what values I need to honor in my life plan.

Mentoring ⌁ June 27

"What an elder sees sitting, the young can't see standing."

—Ibo proverb

Whom would you name as a mentor in your life? And whom do *you* mentor? Mentoring can be formal or informal—some participate in mentoring programs; others simply rely on the help of others.

Bill had been raised with strong messages of "do it yourself." His family thought it weak to need help and that you were a "wimp" if you needed to *ask* for help. Bill had done well in his career in the retail business, but when he was put in charge of a new technological division, he knew he was in over his head. He decided to break his family "rule" and ask for mentoring. He worked closely with Tim, a senior person in technology, and was amazed at how well they connected and how much he learned. When Bill had questions, he called Tim. As a result of this positive experience, Bill set up a structured mentoring program for his group.

Just for today, I will appreciate the mentors in my life and identify where I am mentoring others.

June 28 ~ *Mindfulness*

"He did each single thing as if he did nothing else."

—Charles Dickens

Mindfulness is the art of giving your full and undivided attention to what you are doing, even if you're only walking up the steps. When you're being mindful, you're aware of the sound of your footsteps, the pace you're walking at, the pictures on the wall, and the smell of the stairwell. You are fully present. You are not thinking about the report you have to write, only about walking up the steps.

How do you practice mindfulness in your daily work life? How do you remind yourself that being mindful helps you work more productively, more efficiently, and with far less stress?

Julie knew her position would be high stress when she accepted it, but she didn't realize how little time she would have for reflection at work. When a friend gave Julie some books on mindfulness, she decided to take a "health day" to sit at home in silence and read her books. Afterward, she took time each day for a walking meditation in her office. She practiced deep breathing while walking slowly, exhaling every other step. Julie learned to use this to test how balanced she felt; her body did not lie to her. She practiced being mindful throughout her day and soon found she came home with energy for her family.

Just for today, I will be conscious of my mindfulness. I will take time to breathe and nurture my spirit.

"The mind ought sometimes to be diverted that it may return to better thinking."

—Phaedrus

How do you find renewal in your work life? There are two kinds of renewal at work. First, we can change our work patterns and routines. Of course, our businesses may demand that some areas stay consistent, but we can usually find at least some small parts of our day that can be changed and thus renewed. Second, we can renew ourselves through spirit-filling activities. Some employees take a few days off for a vacation, or even a work sabbatical, but many find other simple ways to renew themselves. One small group in a company takes daily walks before work, exploring new parts of their city. Others use music to restore themselves. Some employees play Frisbee at lunchtime.

Karen considered quitting her job; she was bored. Yet her benefits and pension plan were hard to leave. At a friend's suggestion, she made a long list of renewal activities and began them. Within months, she was satisfied.

Just for today, I will find ways to renew my work patterns and to renew myself. I will do something physical or use aesthetics to fill my senses.

June 30 ⁓ *Wholeness*

"We are whole beings. We know this somewhere in a part of ourselves that feels like memory."

—Susan Griffin

What does wholeness mean to you? Is it just an abstract concept to you, or is it something real in your life? Bringing our whole selves to work means acknowledging our physical, mental, and emotional sides at work. Oft-heard terms such as "touchy-feely" certainly block some people from being "whole" at work.

One company's human resources (HR) department decided to develop a wholeness initiative. Jenny, the vice president, had been fearful to work with the HR director on this initiative; her banking background saw it as "fluff." Within six months, however, Jenny was totally on board. She recognized the energy gained in the workplace when employees had permission to bring their whole selves to work. The entire company seemed more relaxed; outsiders who entered commented on the warmth extended to them. The head of the company's cultural diversity program said this was a major achievement in recognizing diversity. Interestingly, this fresh approach to relationships at work also correlated with greater profits.

Just for today, I will bring my wholeness to my work. I have the right to be fully human in all of my life.

July

Justice ～ July 1

"Justice is truth in action."

—Benjamin Disraeli

What does justice look like? To what degree is it fairness; to what degree is it righting a wrong?

Janice was excited in her new role as divisional marketing director with a highly respected firm. The CEO, not the division head, had hired her. During the first month, she felt an importance she had never known before. Within two months, however, the balloon burst— she lost two clients. Janice struggled. Feedback from her division head left her feeling unsafe and sabotaged. She was ashamed and feared being fired.

The CEO and division head called her in to let her know she was in over her head; "perhaps the job is too big" was the message. The CEO knew that justice was key. He knew he was partly responsible because he'd hired her without consulting the division head. They laid out a plan for Janice's development, giving her support and guidance. Janice wept in gratitude. Within a year, she was solidly on track.

Just for today, I will ask where I am involved in acts of justice and what justice I observe in my work world.

July 2 〜 *Self-Doubt*

"Just trust yourself, then you will know how to live."

—Johann Wolfgang von Goethe

When was the last time you faced self-doubt? Do you know what triggered it? It is natural to experience self-doubt. Often we know self-doubt through our interactions with others.

Mary was very successful as a production assistant in an advertising agency and was well liked. She was also confident. When Pete joined the agency in the production department, the creative group cheered. Pete was widely known for his design work and had a fine reputation. Immediately, something sprang forth in Mary—the dragon of self-doubt. Mary realized that she was comparing her insides to Pete's confident outsides and that this was unhealthy. She tried positive self-talk, which was somewhat helpful. Her sister reminded her that her brother and his accomplishments used to trigger a similar reaction: Mary felt that her special place in the family was threatened. When Mary recognized that Pete was not her brother, she began to make positive comments about him. Within a short time, her self-doubt faded and her self-confidence returned.

Just for today, I will review my self-doubt and ask myself what might be triggering that feeling. I will accept myself as I am, and I will allow others to be as they are.

"I never know what I think about something until I read what I've written on it."

—William Faulkner

How do you use writing at work? Writing can be an important tool in the workplace. If you are new in your position, I encourage you to journal all your immediate observations and feelings. You will never have that clarity about the system again—you soon become an "insider." Writing can also be used to clarify your thinking. By using the right brain, we access the creative unconscious. Our left brain can help the nonlinear side to order priorities and make decisions, giving us "whole brain management."

John felt emotionally reactive to his colleague, Nick, at least twice a week. John knew he was being irrational and that it was not entirely about Nick. He obsessed with angry feelings, yet he did not want to behave inappropriately when asking Nick for work. John took his boss's suggestion of using writing to express his feelings. In a notebook he kept in the back of his desk drawer, John recorded his feelings about working with Nick and what he wanted to say to him. John was soon able to communicate with Nick in a most appropriate tone, while exploring the source of his reaction to Nick.

Just for today, I will use my "personal assistant," my writing, to help me clarify my thinking. Writing can also serve as an "admission" center for my honest observations and feelings.

July 4 ∽ *Intimidation*

"Nothing is more despicable than respect based on fear."

—Albert Camus

How have you experienced intimidation in your workplace—as an observer or a recipient?

Charles was unaware of his intimidating style. Tall, white haired, and distinguished looking, his very appearance could intimidate many. Charles had a high IQ and a mind quicker than most around him. Despite Charles's many strengths, a new vice president in the company asked him to get some coaching for his communication style. Charles agreed.

Observing Charles in action during a meeting, the coach noted Charles was impatient and pushed for agreement. He saw strong nonverbal "push away" messages (e.g., arms crossed over his chest and pointing fingers) and the group deferring to Charles. When Charles asked the coach for feedback after the meeting, the coach was honest and asked him if he had any idea of how intimidating he was. The shocked initial response of "No, I have never heard that!" seemed believable to the coach. Charles was unaware of how he was coming across to others but wanted to become aware. The coach gave him feedback on his strong nonverbal behaviors, and Charles began paying more attention to his actions.

Just for today, I will become conscious of how I treat others.

"Don't be afraid of the space between your dreams and reality. If you can dream it, you can make it so."

—Belva Davis

Is your dream for your future materializing for you? Are you following your dream? Or have you not allowed yourself to have a dream?

To make our dreams come true, we need to envision them and carry them in our minds. I asked a group of executives I was working with to write down their dreams and then envision where they would be in one year in relation to their dreams. This was a letter they were writing to themselves, dated one year out. The executives wrote how they saw themselves progressing toward their dream and talking about it with others; they also described how they were feeling about it. After writing earnestly and eagerly for at least twenty minutes, they then folded the letters and put them in self-addressed envelopes that I would mail back to them in a year. When they received their letters a year later, many called immediately to let me know that they had read them aloud and indeed had made progress.

Just for today, I will assess the progress on my dream. If I don't have one, I will give myself permission to envision one.

July 6 ∼ *Knowing*

"What you hear you forget, what you see you remember, what you do you know."

—Chinese proverb

How do you know what you know? Knowing is the deepest form of knowledge; it lies deep within us and comes from our experiences. Knowing is a combination of our intuition, our values, our information base, and our action. An old Sufi saying is "If you have not experienced it, it simply is not true." We make our best decisions when they're based on our knowing.

Betty had to make a major decision for her firm: knowing the high failure rate of mergers, should they move forward with the offer that was on the table? Betty did her research. After learning that the companies' values seemed aligned—and becoming excited about the new enterprise and trusting her gut knowing—she said "yes." Five years later, Betty felt good when the merged company celebrated another anniversary. She smiled when she reviewed her decision-making process, which was to trust her gut knowing. She was grateful for her spiritual trust.

Just for today, I will trust my knowing. Becoming informed and getting in touch with my feelings will help me make sound decisions.

"The purpose of life is not to get rid of the butterflies in your stomach, but to make them fly in formation."

—Author unknown

Did you know that your anxiety can help you at work? Anxieties are a signal; they are a warning system within us, saying "Halt!" "Look!" "Listen!" Our anxieties are either honest fears or old, familiar feelings we have carried irrationally from our past. If our anxieties come from legitimate fears, we can face them honestly and move beyond them.

I like to think of anxiety as lying at the threshold of change. Often we feel anxiety when we are entering a new position, a new workplace, or a new experience. These anxieties are natural; they are telling us that we care about our performance. However, when we carry anxieties from our past, such as those that come from old stories of self-doubt, we face a challenge of another kind. We must trace the history of these anxieties and find the primary sources. These anxieties often hover about, leading us to a dead end. We can move through these anxieties by respecting and working on them instead of burying them. Otherwise, they will continue to haunt us.

Just for today, I will listen to my anxious feelings and ask myself whether they are legitimate anxieties from the present or hovering haunts that have been hiding in my closet.

July 8 ⁓ *Life Energy*

"Nothing ever succeeds which exuberant spirits have not helped to produce."

—Friedrich Wilhelm Nietzsche

How frequently do you see life energy at work? Life energy is a powerful, vibrant, positive force that can lead people in new directions. And it is contagious.

Recently, I used guided imagery when helping a group of managers on their visions of upcoming management changes. Todd, the assistant store manager, was negative. He saw himself driving a school bus loaded with passengers who were all asleep. Todd said, "I am doing all the driving and I have to get them where they are going." Todd's colleague Jack replied, "Well, I see us as a group of climbers, ascending a not-too-steep mountain. We are all roped together, assisting one another up toward the summit." "And with enthusiasm," he quickly added. To this, Todd replied, "Well you have a lot more hope than I do!" Jack said, "I'll carry the enthusiasm and hope initially if you will carry it when you see us making progress!" "Sure, I can do that," replied Todd. Within months, all of the group members were on their new climb; Jack's energy had ignited them. Todd joined in, with hope. They climbed successfully and gradually implemented the changes.

Just for today, I will allow my exuberance to shine. I will not apologize for my life energy.

"When you cease to make a contribution, you begin to die."

—Eleanor Roosevelt

Do you have a sense of how you make a difference at work? Few of us are going to make a great invention or create the world's next technological advance, yet indeed we can make a difference!

When Louise's son was diagnosed with leukemia and was given two months to live, Louise did not know where to turn. She needed extensive support. Her extended family lived far away and could not travel to help her with her home care. Her husband already worked two jobs to make ends meet. At the hospital where she worked, Louise's co-workers gathered together to see what they could do. They devised a plan to carry Louise's workload by extending their own hours. They worked out their schedules and went to their manager for approval. Louise sobbed with gratitude when she learned that she could stay at home with her son and that her work was fully covered. Louise's work friends truly made a difference in their hour-by-hour commitment to Louise.

Just for today, I will ask myself how and where I have made a difference and how and where I can still make a difference.

July 10 ∽ *Silence*

"Silence first makes us pilgrims. Secondly silence guards the fire within. Thirdly, silence teaches us how to speak."

—Henri Nouwen

How does silence enter your work world? In a highly stimulating environment, how do you make room to sit in silence and learn from the awareness that comes from quieting your mind? To know what we really know, we need to go inside the silence.

After a long, hard month at work, I attended a silent retreat. For the first days of the nine-day retreat, my mind seemed to be JFK Airport—something took off and landed about every minute. Then it happened; I could truly sit in silence and see what reflections brought me. I had never realized how much energy it took to talk! The awareness brought about by peaceful silence was new for me. Upon my return home, I committed to taking a small amount of time daily for silence, for reflection. We can do this almost anywhere, although you may need to remove yourself temporarily if you work in a crowded area surrounded by stimulating sounds and voices. Developing the discipline of silence makes room for the "fire within" to ignite our spirits.

Just for today, I will take time for silence. I will listen to the silence and see what it offers me.

"When patterns are broken, new worlds can emerge."

—Tuli Kupferberg

Have you ever experienced a cultural shift at your workplace—a time when the company's values were being assessed and redefined? Living through a cultural shift is like changing the direction of your sailing ship. Not all ships take a direct "tack"; some take a slower approach, gradually and subtly changing direction.

When Lloyd joined his firm as CEO, he knew of its reputation for "sleazy" management with cutthroat business tactics. The shocking behaviors of the former CEO were known throughout the industry. Lloyd knew the cultural shift he wanted to lead would take time. He also knew that dramatically changing the environment would include struggles, with some people leaving. Lloyd was committed, however. He led a cultural change process that started with the senior management team and extended all the way down to the plants, working on communication and self-awareness skills. Lloyd was right; there were struggles and some employees left. Over a five-year period, the company made a substantial investment in training, but Lloyd recognized that indeed the culture had shifted—to a culture of respect.

Just for today, I will examine how I'm helping my work culture shift. I will act with behaviors that fit in a culture of respect.

July 12 ～ *Fundamentals of Feelings*

"Feeling is more fundamental than thinking; feeling gives rise to thinking, which gives rise to action."

—Kevin Cashman

Our feelings give us access to our true spirits—our creativity, our ability to connect with others, and our source of self-worth. Buried feelings, like neglected vegetables stored in our refrigerators, eventually create rot and decay—or they explode.

Maria reported that she never felt angry. Yet her work colleagues saw her as an angry person and gave her that feedback in an assessment form. In a company training seminar, the leader asked the participants to write about an event in their lives that they thought still troubled them. Maria wrote her story rapidly and many feelings surfaced, including betrayal, deep hurt, and hot anger. As she wrote, Maria wondered whether others could see her anger; she felt herself burning inside. When she told friends about it at lunch, she received empathy and compassion. Maria then wrote a letter to the person who betrayed her; that person was dead, but Maria's feelings were not. Within months, Maria's friends and family told her how differently they experienced her. She seemed more open and creative.

Just for today, I will accept that my feelings just are and I shall not judge them. I will consider how my feelings drive my behavior and actions.

Procrastination ~ July 13

"Accomplish the great task by a series of small acts."

—Lao Tzu

Are you a procrastinator? What areas do you procrastinate in? What happens to your self-esteem when you procrastinate? Procrastination guarantees feelings of guilt, inadequacy, and defensiveness.

Dennis was a high-energy person; he enthusiastically volunteered for any project available. But Dennis was a procrastinator, and this eventually caught up with him. Dennis had offered to plan his company's divisional meeting, which was to be held in a major convention city. He didn't get around to making hotel meeting arrangements for a while, however; when he finally got to work, he discovered there were no rooms available! He knew the other travel plans had been arranged. He now had consequences to face for overextending himself. Regretfully, Dennis called a meeting and took responsibility for what had happened; he apologized for the high prices his co-workers paid for his procrastination. He heard their feelings and made a promise to himself. This promise led Dennis to stop procrastinating; he learned to set limits. Today he is grateful for his life-changing experience.

Just for today, I will take care of my "to do" list and will not procrastinate. If I am overcommitted, I will turn over work rather than procrastinate.

July 14 ～ Outsiders

"We are partakers of a common nature, and the same causes that contribute to the benefit of one contribute to the benefit of another."

—William Godwin

Who are the outsiders in your workplace? How would you describe them? Does it seem that they do not want to be involved? Or perhaps you feel like an outsider yourself. At times, most of us enter into that zone where we simply feel outside the work circle, distanced from others.

Sharon noticed that John seemed outside her work group. Although the group was friendly, the other members shared a long history and talk of the past often left John feeling like an outsider. Sharon met with her group one day when John was absent and asked them to tell stories of when they felt like outsiders. She then talked about the shared responsibility for John's inclusion, asking the group whether they would be willing to stay in the present in their social talk so that John could join their current history. Enough members of the group did make that accommodation; they saved their history for other times, and within months John was no longer an outsider.

Just for today, I will acknowledge the outsiders I see and reach out to them. I will also ask myself when I have felt like an outsider at work.

"If you're totally committed to something, the discipline comes easy. When you're there—when you're all there."

—Sharon Wood

How would you rate yourself on a discipline scale from one to ten, with ten being high? Our discipline is the glue for our commitments. Recently, a group of employees whose work involved sitting most of the day committed to physical exercise. Each member of the group took on walking or running as a discipline and committed to three days a week, minimum. They were highly energetic when reporting in to one another about their newfound discipline. One group member, Ted, was very overweight; the other employees asked how they could help him. Ted admitted he was uncertain about following through with the walking commitment, as he was not very disciplined in most areas of his life. Immediately Barry said, "Well, Ted, we live near one another; let's run together, starting with just a mile!" Ted reluctantly took Barry up on the offer. Within three months, Ted and Barry ran a ten-kilometer race. Ted was proud of his reward for the discipline, but more than that, he now changed his work patterns to reflect this newfound ally—discipline.

Just for today, I will rate myself on a discipline scale and make whatever adjustments are needed to enjoy the satisfaction and the rewards of discipline.

July 16 ⌒ *Persistence*

"If you get up one more time than you fall, you will make it through."

—Chinese proverb

Persistence pays, and staying true to our course means that we can focus on and gain both short- and long-term rewards.

Jo-Anne had received a very critical review at her new job; her former long-term employer had never provided any feedback because she was so good with financial matters and brought in good revenues. Now, Jo-Anne was faced with peer and subordinate feedback that indicated she was unwilling to ask for help, defensive about receiving criticism, and arrogant in her leadership. Shocked and fearful, Jo-Anne wrote her own contract for behavioral changes and reviewed it with her senior manager. She had a short, but difficult list. She committed to seeking and listening to others' opinions and feedback. Jo-Anne was persistent in her new pledge. She kept a daily record, marking off her new behaviors. Within weeks people were murmuring, "Have you noticed Jo-Anne lately?"

Just for today, I will ask where I am being persistent in my work and what the desired goals are for this commitment.

"It is a little embarrassing that, after forty-five years of research and study, the best advice I can give to people is to be a little kinder to each other."

—Aldous Huxley

Have you ever observed the quality of managerial etiquette in your workplace? Do the members of the management team display good manners and respect in their interactions?

Once when called into a business, I was struck by the beauty of the offices—the rich mahogany woods and leathers in their furniture—and their top-floor suite. The executives wore monogrammed shirts under their costly Italian suits. Somehow, I expected their behavior to be as dignified as their appearance. I could not have been more wrong! I learned that the senior management gossiped heavily, both among themselves and about one another to their employees. If they wanted to force someone to agree with them, they would send an e-mail to the entire group, rather than speaking personally to one another. The top management here was lacking in managerial etiquette. When I named it, they seemed surprised; they said they had never heard the term. In our work together, the managers told stories of early childhood disrespect. We developed a code of conduct that slowly began to shift the system.

Just for today, I will assess my own etiquette as well as that of others in my work environment. I will walk my talk in my own workplace behaviors.

July 18 ⌒ *Hopelessness*

"As long as we have hope, we have direction, the energy to move, and the map to move by. We have a hundred alternatives, a thousand paths, and an infinity of dreams. Hopeful, we are halfway to where we want to go; hopeless, we are lost forever."

—Hong Kong proverb

Have you ever felt hopeless at your work? Many human resource directors are attempting to address the hopelessness that employees experience when major layoffs are announced. Hopelessness can spread through the system like a virus; it seems to be in the air and affects even those who are staying with the firm.

One major technology firm recently made a unique offering to the eighty thousand employees it was cutting. The company contracted with a career consulting firm to offer each employee a class in resume writing and career planning. Although the company could no longer offer them jobs, it gave its employees something practical to take with them; the employees felt grateful for this exit gift. Many had been long-term employees and felt truly hopeless; some had never before had a resume. By focusing on the work history they had gained over the years, some felt renewed spirits in going forward.

Just for today, I will focus on any pockets of hopelessness in my workplace, whether in individuals or in work groups, and look for the glimmer of hope that change can bring.

"Deep within us is a creative spirit desiring to be free, and we may as well get out of its way, for it will give us no peace until we do."

—Mary Richards

Just how would you describe a spirited leader? Could that be you?

Charlotte was a bit uncertain about how she would be received when she joined a financial firm as the vice president of human resources. It was an old, established company with very dignified, long-term employees. Most of the executives were male. When she interviewed with the search committee, the group assured her that she would have the freedom she needed to create a "spirited workplace." Charlotte was warm, energetic, natural, and liked people. Her door was open. Yet Charlotte knew she had to walk slowly to bring the concept of "spirit" into work. She recalled the story about renowned anthropologist Margaret Mead. When told she could not bring her walking stick into museums, Mead tucked it under her cape as she entered. Charlotte understood that she must carry her flame slowly so that employees could discover it for themselves. Over time, by developing trust with all her co-workers, her enthusiasm spread, and the firm formed a "spirited leadership" circle.

Just for today, I will ask myself how I am nurturing my creative spirit and holding the candle to ignite someone else's.

July 20 ～ *Self-Pity*

"There are few human emotions as warm, comforting, and enveloping as self-pity. And nothing is more corrosive and destructive. There is only one answer; turn away from it and move on."

—Dr. Megan Reik

Have you ever worked with someone who indulged in self-pity?

George felt self-pity when his friends were promoted to full professors; he had been an associate professor for many years. His colleagues saw him as fragile. In a faculty development seminar, Janice, the leader, noticed this and learned from the chair that George felt it was too personal an issue to discuss. "I think George needs to learn how his self-pity is holding him back," Janice replied. "Well, please go for it!" said the chair.

Janice used humor and teasing in giving the faculty feedback in the seminar. Toward the end of the seminar, Janice said, "George, it is time for you to put that self-pitying little kid in you down for a nap and get on with your life!" First a hush spread as the group froze with tension, and then George burst out laughing. "Why, I did not know anyone knew; and I had never considered that," he exclaimed. Within months, George's co-workers saw the difference; because of feedback, George was letting go of his self-pity.

Just for today, I will ask myself when and how I meet self-pity—in myself and in others. I will admit that self-pity holds me back.

"One of the symptoms of approaching nervous breakdown is the belief that one's work is terribly important."

—Bertrand Russell

D o you ever feel your life is out of control? Recently, a large magazine survey revealed that more than 50 percent of American workers feel out of control.

When Lynn went to work on Wall Street, she learned it was "normal" to work seventeen-hour days. Late in the day, a gourmet dining cart was wheeled in ("just in case you need to stay a bit!"), and the analysts stayed until 2 A.M. ("in case you might need them"). A company car service drove employees home.

After three months of this, Lynn took three days off to rest at home. She assessed her life: she had not seen her women friends socially for three months; she had ignored her husband; and she had missed an old family friend's funeral. Worst of all, her preschool son and only child had made a Christmas wish list with "I want my mommy" at the top. Lynn saw that her life was out of control. She renegotiated her work contract to create a forty-five-hour workweek, for less money.

Just for today, I will assess the "control" factor in my life—how much time I have for my personal relationships, my reading, and my time for renewal. I may need to make changes.

July 22 ⁓ *Community*

"No one can whistle a symphony. It takes an orchestra to play it."

—H. E. Luccock

Does your workplace offer a feeling of community? With employees sharing a common interest and working toward a common goal, community can be created at work.

Long frustrated in his job, Rob saw something he had never noticed before: as people entered his workplace, they stood in line waiting for the elevators to take them to their contemporary lush office suites—but no one spoke to one another. He knew something had been missing; now he finally named it. Because he yearned for a sense of community at work, Rob decided to leave. He knew he spent too much time at work not to feel a sense of community.

Rob was careful in his selection of a new job. Before he signed on with a new firm, he spent an hour on two different mornings sitting in the lobby and observing employees entering the office. He saw people chatting, inquiring about one another, laughing. Rob read the cues accurately; he joined a company that had a true sense of community with remarkably loyal employees.

Just for today, I will ask myself how I experience community in my work. For some of us it is readily available; those who work solo need to create a work community with colleagues.

"All my life through, the new sights of nature made me rejoice like a child."

—Marie Curie

Do you have any contact with nature in your workplace? Paying attention to the natural world helps us restore our spirits. Whether you work in a concrete jungle or a rural setting, you can always walk outside and look up at the cloud patterns in the sky.

Researcher Rachel Kaplan did a study that revealed that office workers with a view of nature liked their jobs more, enjoyed better health, and reported greater life satisfaction. Joyce knew that something was missing in her work world. The fluorescent lights, the gray walls, and the square acoustical tile ceilings brought her spirits down. She originally went to her office manager and requested that the company hire a service to bring plants in monthly. When she learned that the company could not afford this, Joyce went to a local florist and bought several plants that did not require high natural light and lived well with fluorescent lights. With just this bit of nature in her immediate surroundings, Joyce's spirits lifted; others in the company followed suit.

Just for today, I will focus on nature in my work life. There is nothing to stop me from bringing some small corner of the natural world into work.

July 24 ～ *Attention*

Do you find it easy to focus your attention when at work? Years ago, philosopher and psychologist William James wrote about two kinds of attention. The first kind of attention is directed, very focused, and leads to fatigue. The other attention, known as fascination and curiosity, leads to uplifting the spirit.

Ron worked with numbers all day; he was responsible for providing all kinds of data for reports, monthly and annually. Although he excelled at his job, he was beginning to become burned out and fatigued from the pressure. Ron, through some conversations with friends, decided to make some changes. He still had to use concentrated attention to fulfill his job duties, but he also took time to look into numbers he was simply curious about. For example, he was curious about percentages of employee retention and diversity, and he wanted to "run numbers" on how different costs broke down. When he took the time to explore these areas, he was able to compare what happened when they hired a new employee rather than invest in retraining current employees. Ron no longer felt fatigued; his fascination attention anchored him in his work.

Just for today, I will ask myself how much of my day is spent in directed attention or fascination attention.

"We want people to feel with us more than to act for us."

—George Eliot

Have you ever considered the role of empathy at work? Empathy refers to the ability to identify with the feelings and thoughts of others, to vicariously experience what they are going through. Empathy skills can be taught and help ignite the spirit at work. Empathy can be extremely powerful. When we learn to listen empathically, our co-workers feel heard; that is the only goal of empathy. I coach people to use phrases such as "It sounds like . . ."; this is a tool that helps us listen for the music behind the words and offer our interpretation to the concerned person.

Bonnie had thought that hearing someone meant it was her responsibility not only to find the solution, but also to take it on personally. This caused her to create distances. When she learned to empathize—internalizing the message "empathy before strategy"—she was seen as a more effective leader. She also found that her new empathy skills carried over into her home life and resulted in her family members feeling truly heard.

Just for today, I will focus on my empathic listening. Am I taking the time to truly listen empathically to others?

July 26 ～ *Disclosure*

"Be honorable with yourself if you wish to associate with honorable people."

—Welsh proverb

How free do you feel to disclose your true thoughts and feelings to others at work?

Zoe had felt troubled; her supervisors had told her she was going to be promoted, but she could not tell her co-workers until a new company plan was revealed to all employees. Zoe had two close women friends at work and wondered whether they could tell that she was holding a secret. She also wondered how they would respond to her good news. Although Zoe felt loyal to her supervisor's request, she felt even more loyal to her friends. Whenever the subject of the new plan came up, Zoe wondered whether they could read her. When the secret began to interfere with her work, Zoe went to her supervisor with her dilemma. They agreed that she could tell her two friends *with the expectation for total confidence.* Zoe felt deep relief after disclosing her secret to her friends; they were both happy for Zoe. Zoe's friends proved that personal trust can be honored at work.

Just for today, I will ask myself whether there is anything I need to disclose to anyone. I will pay attention to anyone who is trying to disclose trusted information to me.

"I can't change the direction of the wind, but I can adjust my sails to always reach my destination."

—Jimmy Dean

Have you ever lost a job? Anne could not see it coming. Her reviews had been excellent; she felt good about her track record from her twelve years with the company. The new department head had said he would not make any drastic changes. Within two weeks after his arrival, however, Anne was told that her job was eliminated and the work folded into a new position. Anne was devastated, fighting back the tears. She felt lost, angry, and betrayed. How would she tell people? In her mid-forties, she wondered who would want her.

Through her church, Anne found a group for people in transition and slowly began the climb through the shame. With the group's support, she gradually saw how her work crisis had led to spiritual growth. When Anne went out on job interviews, she was renewed, buoyed up by a caring support system, and filled with confidence that her job loss was not about her personal competencies or personality, but rather about a change in leadership.

Just for today, I will be sensitive to those who have lost their positions and be supportive of their struggles.

"There is no passion so contagious as that of fear."

—Michel Eyquem de Montaigne

How do you see "games" in your workplace? Are you engaged in some knowingly? *Games* refers to those unspoken, implicit agreements that people engage in to avoid conflict and the risk of not being liked. The most successful of firms can be entrenched in game playing.

Cheryl, the top female executive in her firm, was proud of how her all-woman team worked together. When she proposed structural changes, however, she stepped on a land mine of buried feelings. She learned the group members had not been honest with her. Their game was "I won't confront you if you won't confront me." Cheryl sought help from human resources. The HR facilitator helped her unmask the games. Cheryl learned she had a fear-driven group; each person in the group revealed what her fears were. During this process, Cheryl learned to read people more clearly and to ask for feedback about their decision making. After a two-month period of honest feedback, the group's trust increased greatly and together the members helped Cheryl carry out her new organizational structure.

Just for today, I will pay attention to any games that I play. I will ask myself what I fear in being honest at work.

"A candle loses nothing by lighting another candle."

—Father James Keller

Have you ever worked for a company that promotes helping—outside its walls as well as within?

Jeanine felt proud to work for her company. The company's president, Billy Weisman, and his key management team valued helping others in the community and all employees received time off to volunteer. Throughout the year, employees were recognized and honored for the help they gave to one another and the community. What the employees did not realize, however, was that their contributions throughout the city were occasionally being videotaped.

At an all-company breakfast, employees were shown the video that depicted various volunteer projects. Tears flowed as the employees realized the impact of their total contribution—they had helped children, people who were homeless, and those with chronic illness, to name just a few. The employees felt connected with their co-workers. At the end of the breakfast, each person received a clock engraved with the message "Helping makes your spirit soar." This experience had an effect for many months to come.

Just for today, I will ask myself how I am truly "helping" at work—whether inside or outside the organization.

July 30 ⌒ *Mind Invasion*

"Nothing is at last sacred but the integrity of your own mind."

—Ralph Waldo Emerson

Have you ever felt someone trying to "get into" your head, your mind? Such mind invasion involves an interrogator asking questions rather than disagreeing outright. The goal is for you to adopt the other person's thoughts.

Ben often used the telephone when he engaged in mind invading; he did not have to face his victims. Ted had experienced Ben's invasions for several years and was tired of it; he felt indirectly attacked and was determined to protect himself. Soon, Ben called Ted and said, "Don't you wonder if you are getting overly involved with that project?" He followed with a barrage of pointed questions. This time Ted spoke up. "Ben," he firmly stated, "I surely wish that you would give me your opinions directly, rather than trying to get into my head to have me feed back what you want to hear!" Ben was shocked and speechless for a minute. He then confessed that he did this quite often and was aware of what he was doing. Ben agreed to stop invading Ted in that way, and they created a mutually respectful relationship.

Just for today, I will pay attention to any tendencies I might have to "get into" someone else's head. I will also recognize when someone is invading me.

"Though we travel the world over to find the beautiful, we must carry it with us or we find it not."

—Ralph Waldo Emerson

Do you travel for your job? If so, how do you take care of yourself when traveling? Many see work travel as glamorous with fine dining and luxury hotels, rather than stress-filled days of cancelled flights and lonely meals in hotel dining rooms.

Jacqueline's job required travel. Single, she loved her work but recently was beginning to feel ungrounded. Some mornings she awoke not knowing where she was, and it took some time for her to feel present. She was beginning to feel disconnected from her home life. One day when checking her voice mail, Jacqueline heard a message from her four-year-old niece, which began with "Hi, Auntie Jackie—I'm coloring!" Upon hearing her niece's voice, Jacqueline felt her shoulders come down and her muscles seemed to relax throughout her whole body. She smiled; she had just discovered a new stress reliever. Whenever she felt ungrounded, she now called home to hear her simple, loving message from her niece. Her heart connection grounded her.

Just for today, I will focus on how I can ground myself when traveling. I will create new ways to relieve my travel stress.

August

〰〰

"Good fortune is what happens when opportunity meets with planning."

—Thomas Edison

How effectively do you plan your work? Do you create a timetable and then revise as you go?

Kathleen worked in corporate communication; she was spontaneous, hard working, and well liked. Her co-workers teased her about being "right brained" and had learned to accommodate her nonplanning style. But one day, Kathleen's lack of preparation became a serious problem. She had agreed to write a speech that Jim, the executive vice president, would be giving on Sunday night at the opening of a company-wide retreat. Jim left town during the week, confident that Kathleen would have the speech in good shape for the retreat. Upon his return on Friday night, however, he was shocked to learn that Kathleen had not budgeted time to write the speech and had prepared nothing at all. After receiving an angry call from Jim, she reacted by slapping together a speech overnight. Jim was very disappointed when he read the speech Saturday morning. It was intellectually sloppy, not typical of Kathleen's work. After hours of editing, he called Kathleen again and told her that her future was now on the line. This was a turning point for Kathleen; she learned that she needed to push herself to make sure she got her planning done, despite her natural tendencies.

Just for today, I will plan my work. By doing so, I will be relaxed in knowing that I am organized and ready for what lies ahead.

August 2 ⁓ *Workaholism*

"Some to dance, some to make bonfires, each man to what sport and revels his addiction leads him."

—William Shakespeare

Workaholism is cunning; it is very rewarding. Eddie knew about alcoholism from his family history, and he did not drink at all. He loved his work and was very successful in running his family business. But gradually, he began to spend more and more time working. He took telephone calls at home until midnight; before long, his wife, Sheila, began to feel increasingly estranged. As the workaholism deepened, Sheila observed similarities to the pattern in Eddie's first marriage: his first wife, complaining of loneliness, divorced him. Sheila began attending a program for spouses of alcoholics; substituting the word *working* for *drinking* in everything she heard, Sheila was shocked to see how closely Eddie's patterns paralleled those of an alcoholic. When she described to Eddie what she had discovered, he was horrified. He realized he might lose a second woman he loved. Eddie started attending a men's group for Adult Children of Alcoholics and faced the buried pain he had been running from throughout his life.

Just for today, I will ask myself whether I have workaholic tendencies; have my choices made for a rich personal life? If necessary, I will seek help for my behavior.

"Work has been undergoing perhaps its most significant transformation since Americans left the farm for the factory a century ago."
—Daniel H. Pink

Are you self-employed? While some choose to work alone, many such people are not self-employed by choice. Rather, many have been "outplaced" or are hired as "independent contractors" by companies who want to avoid paying benefits. Whether by choice or not, working for oneself offers numerous opportunities for growth—both in skill development and self-esteem and empowerment.

Dennis had no idea there would be so many lessons ahead for him when he quit his job and struck out on his own. Even though Dennis's consulting skills were in demand, he faced strong competition—from the major firms as well as from his colleagues. Now Dennis faced his greatest challenge: he had to market himself, something that didn't come naturally to him. Previously, all his work had been handed to him through his company. For almost two years he struggled with his self-confidence. But in his new vulnerability, Dennis began to develop spiritually through facing the uncomfortable feelings that came with marketing himself. Over time, marketing himself became a little easier, and his consulting career took off.

Just for today, I will focus on what knowledge I have developed within myself so I can face the challenges of being self-employed.

August 4 ～ *Systems Thinking*

"Chaos and Order combined equal balance."

—Richard Garriott

When we use systems thinking, we see ourselves or our work group as a part of the whole division, company, industry, or professional system. As the old saying goes, the whole is greater than the sum of its parts. With this perspective, we can recognize how interrelated we all are and that the system is never fixed in place—that it is always in the process of seeking balance.

John had never heard the term *systems thinking* when he told his colleagues, "I am worried; these employees withdraw because I promote change." The employees, on the other hand, would likely say, "We withdraw because he is promoting changes." In these statements each blames the other for the position, thus creating stuckness, or a static dynamic. Although both views are really attempts to balance the system in their minds, both actually keep the system stuck. John had to consider the effects of change on the entire work system. He began asking about his own intentions and whether the change was good for future generations. In time, as John made behavioral changes and let go of rigid thinking, his employees walked with him.

Just for today, I will focus on the whole system, what sustains it and what I can do to create a future.

"It is only by labour that thought can be made healthy, and only by thought that labour can be made happy, and the two cannot be separated with impunity."

—John Ruskin

Perhaps it is hard to imagine, in our high-stress lives, the concept of organizational well-being. Usually, our time is invested in our personal well-being. Yet we know that we can move beyond ourselves to create and foster organizational well-being.

Keith had noted for some time that the routine nature of the work in his plant did not allow for much creativity, yet he knew that almost everyone was creative in some way. Keith decided to express his own creativity by bringing in cartoons each day. Soon, others brought them in as well. It was not long before poetry was introduced at the beginning of each staff meeting and graffiti boards were hung throughout the plant. Employees posted their favorite vacation photographs in the cafeteria. Keith felt most successful in fostering organizational well-being when a group of assembly-line workers asked to have music piped into their work area. Contrary to senior management fears, the accident rate went down!

Just for today, I will pay attention to my organization's well-being. Even if I work alone, I will focus on bringing aesthetics into my workplace to enhance well-being.

August 6 ～ *Entrepreneurship*

"Go make a footprint in the sands of time. . . . [it] matters not whether the footprint you leave behind is small or large. The important thing is that it has your name inscribed on it."

—William L. Harrell

During the past few decades more than 90 percent of all new jobs came from the entrepreneurial sector. Entrepreneurs are risk takers, and by taking risks, they make things happen. Is there an entrepreneur in you?

Leslie had worked for large corporations before leaving to create her own building-design firm. She and some partners wanted to test an idea and had no trouble finding investors to finance start-up operations. The first year had ups and downs—but mostly downs—and Leslie became scared about her livelihood. At the end of the year, it looked as if they could not pay back their creditors on schedule. When a slick and sleazy businessman wanted to buy in, the group was torn. Some felt that they had to accept the businessman's offer, but Leslie knew that terror invited temptation. She trusted that her self-esteem was the anchor for her risk-taking endeavors and knew what would happen if she yielded. Leslie spoke firmly and honestly about honoring their entrepreneurial spirits and their integrity, and the group came up with a successful alternate plan that didn't compromise their values.

Just for today, I will recognize that entrepreneurship requires a deep faith in oneself and one's abilities. Although risk taking is scary, I will adhere to my fundamental beliefs.

"Honesty is the first chapter in the book of wisdom."

—Thomas Jefferson

Many employees have difficulty dealing with chronic illness in the workplace, illness that affects either themselves or their co-workers.

When he discovered he was HIV-infected, Nick was fearful of the consequences at his office. For several months, he worried about revealing his health status to his employer. His partner was now bedridden, dying of AIDS, and they lived fifteen hundred miles apart; Nick knew his partner needed him. He had to reveal the situation and hope for the best. Nick trembled when he entered his manager's office. After listening carefully, his manager said, "Well I am relieved in a way; I knew something was wrong but did not know what. . . . I am sorry to hear this. How can I help?" Nick was stunned; tears filled his eyes. After further discussion, Nick's manager arranged to transfer him to the large city where his partner lived so they could be together during his partner's last days.

Just for today, I will be sensitive to chronic illness issues that may appear in my work life. I'll remind myself that spirituality at work means bringing the whole self to work, in sickness and in health.

August 8 ～ *People Skills*

"The greatest motivational act one person can do for another is to listen."

—Roy E. Moody

How would you rate your people skills? Author and psychologist Dan Goleman refers to these skills as *social radar*.

Peter, a senior executive who had been with the same company for sixteen years, was known for his people skills; they came naturally to him. Most people referred to him as the "heart" of the organization, and his work was described as "magical." Peter insisted these are learnable, teachable skills. When the company expanded and two of the new regional departments needed Peter's expertise to get up and running, he agreed to take on the challenge but insisted that someone observe and record what constituted "people skills" so that they could use that information in training managers and staff. After six months, Peter and his managers had identified just what this "magic" was: understanding others, listening, empathy, developing potential in others, and service orientation. These skills were not different from the ones identified in Goleman's *Working with Emotional Intelligence;* they are now part of the company's core training curriculums. The positive environment that Peter helped develop influenced the bottom line—the new divisions took off.

Just for today, I will assess my people skills and make a plan to develop areas that need improvement.

"There is no 'I' in TEAM but there is an 'M' and an 'E.'"

—Brian Greco

The Eurocentric heritage of individualism that pervades many workplaces affects our lives and has a cost that many of us do not recognize. Most of us do recognize, however, the value of the millions of dollars spent annually on team building. The notion of teams comes much more naturally to those from areas in the world, such as Asia and Africa, where commitment to the group takes precedence over individuals.

At a team meeting, Muriel, the manager, announced a new position would open soon and wanted to know which members of the team planned to apply. When Ani, a woman from a Tibetan resettlement in Nepal, replied, she said, "Well, I could not consider that until we would see what is best for the team." The rest of the team fell into silence; this was a new concept for them, but it quickly opened up a discussion of what indeed would best serve the team. Muriel felt proud to work with team members who were willing to move away from their individualism.

Just for today, I will ask myself how individualism affects my work life and what the costs are.

August 10 ~ *Humility*

"People with humility don't think less of themselves, they just think of themselves less."

—Ken Blanchard and Norman Vincent Peale

Too often humility is not fully recognized because we are so accustomed to people "honking their own horns." When we live with humility, we recognize that we never do things entirely by ourselves—others are involved in any achievement we might claim.

Sara was a successful businessperson. In addition to her work accomplishments, she had received many awards for her community involvement. Her high energy was obvious, and she seemed to make almost any job look easy. Sara trusted herself; she knew her strengths and weaknesses. Those who worked with her noted that she never spoke about her past accomplishments; she never dropped names, even though she sat on many prestigious national boards. Sara was a reminder that what matters most is knowing and trusting ourselves; with such self-confidence, we can move forward in our work and stop spending energy conveying our importance to others.

Just for today, I will examine my humility and ask myself what challenge I need to face in knowing sincere humility.

"The idea that 'the public interest' supersedes private interests and rights can have but one meaning: that the interests and rights of some individuals take precedence over the interests and rights of others."

—Ayn Rand

Women represent only 10 percent of senior managers in Fortune 500 companies, and less than 4 percent of the CEOs, presidents, executive vice presidents, and COOs are female. Gender inequity today is often underground; the barriers are often insidious.

When Steve and Jack decided they had to face the gender inequities in their company, they examined all their practices and committed themselves to change. First, they had younger men *and* women conduct interviews of job candidates. Second, they extended the interviews from fifteen to forty-five minutes and slowed down the questioning process. Third, they changed the type of questions, asking candidates about qualitative contributions they could make rather than "past financial deals done." This combination of small changes led to their having all the women applicants they could use within nine months! Steve and Jack were pleased with how they could make incremental changes that made a difference.

Just for today, I will reflect on any gender issues at my workplace.

August 12 ～ *Money*

"Real knowledge is to know the extent of one's ignorance."

—Confucius

How do you look at money? How knowledgeable do you feel in understanding financial matters?

Larry had worked hard and was now a high-salaried member of the marketing group in his company. He and his superior had asked me to sit in on some meetings when starting our coaching contract. As the group talked about their budget, profits, and losses, Larry was noticeably silent. Later, he admitted he did not know how to read a profit-and-loss statement. He also admitted how shameful he felt about his carelessness with money in his personal life. He had not invested anything toward his future; he never even balanced his checkbook. When Larry reflected on his childhood, he learned that he had had no money training; he entered into a steep learning curve that not only increased his financial self-esteem, but also allowed him to take his place in his work group.

Just for today, I will focus on money and examine some core beliefs I developed during my childhood that continue to affect my relationship with money.

"If you shut your door to all errors, truth will be shut out."

—Rabindranath Tagore

Being open can be a gift to those around you. How-ever, openness must also be seen in context. We all hear the stories of "airplane intimacy," in which passengers divulge deeply personal information to those sitting next to them. Such openness is usually inconsequential, because it is unlikely the passengers will ever meet again. But in our workplace, we must know what the culture accepts on the openness continuum.

When Sophia was promoted to a management position, it didn't occur to her that she could no longer be as open with her team members. She now belonged to a management team, and sensitive information discussed in management meetings needed to remain confidential. But Sophia continued to discuss information freely with her former peer group. Over time, the group became mistrustful of senior management—including Sophia—and company morale sagged. Eventually, the management team called her on her behavior and told her a boundary had to be drawn. Sophia was shocked; she had never considered that her new role demanded different "rules" regarding openness. With embarrassment, she apologized to both groups and found an appropriate range for her openness.

Just for today, I will focus on my openness. I will ask myself whether I am appropriate in my discussions with clients and colleagues.

August 14 ∽ *Crossing Cultures*

"Harmony exists in difference no less than in likeness, if only the same keynote governs both parts."

—Margaret Fuller

Many cultures are represented in the American workplace today. At work, you will often come in contact with people of backgrounds very different from your own. Some of us even visit other cultures through our jobs.

When Patrick was asked to head a new division in China, he was excited as well as curious to see how the U.S. program would work there. Patrick took a team of four with him to establish a program that would train employees in emotional intelligence—that is, becoming more aware of our emotions in the workplace. When the Americans arrived at the hotel, their hosts met them. Freida, Patrick's colleague, stepped forward and immediately gave each of the Chinese men a big hug. This gesture seemed to alarm them, and they tried to back up. They held their arms out extended, almost rigid, to maintain a distance, common in China with strangers. Freida quickly learned that her attempt to be warm was this culture's boundary invasion.

Just for today, I will consider how cultures outside and inside my workplace differ. I will also attempt to learn more about cultural differences.

"Reality is the things we cannot possibly not know, sooner or later, in one way or another."

—Henry James

It is common for people to deny vulnerable feelings—fear, anxiety, grief, loneliness, need, rejection—feelings that often turn up at work.

Paul, an attorney, was certainly in denial when he began working for a new firm. Though he presented himself well, and many thought he would make partner within a year, others realized that Paul did not read cues well. In time, he alienated clients. Three clients told the firm's owners that they did not want him representing them. Even though he was working in an area of the law that was new for him, Paul denied that he needed help from his more experienced peers. He denied his high anxiety and fear. Paul's employees finally went to the partners and told them their perceptions. When the partners questioned Paul about his work, he spoke in glowing, enthusiastic terms—he was still very much in denial. But the partners would have none of it, and they directed him to get professional help to work through his issues. Paul, now working on a probationary basis, sought help to uncover the feelings he had buried in childhood.

Just for today, I will ask someone I trust what feelings I might be denying.

August 16 ⁓ *Dialogue*

"Good communication is as stimulating as black coffee and just as hard to sleep after."

—Anne Morrow Lindbergh

Do you participate in dialogue in your work? Dialogue, the open exchange of ideas and perspectives, can open the door to deeper levels of understanding.

When Mark learned from his human resources director that the turnover of female employees in their chemical business was extremely high, he decided to find out why. Recognizing that people didn't always reveal the whole truth at exit interviews, Mark called some of the women who had left and arranged to meet with them. At the meeting, Mark heard discouraging stories about how the women were treated regarding salaries and promotions. With this information in hand, he decided to take further action. Mark hired a professional to facilitate a meeting with a group of his senior executives (all white males) and the women who had left. The meeting was built on the process of dialogue—of hearing one another and listening carefully. Mark's dialogue process resulted in a full-blown initiative on diversity; the company worked on hiring and retaining not just women, but people of color as well.

Just for today, I will ask myself where I most recently experienced dialogue in my work. I will look for opportunities to create genuine dialogue.

"The character ethic, which I believe to be the foundation of success, teaches that there are basic principles of effective living, and that people can only experience true success and enduring happiness as they learn and integrate these principles into their basic character."

—Stephen R. Covey

Have you ever faced an ethical dilemma at work? Such situations require knowing your values and having the courage to express your beliefs and feelings honestly.

Sal was proud of his promotion to senior tax account manager; he now handled the taxes of many highly influential, high-profile people. When Sal worked on the taxes of a nationally renowned businessman, he found areas of "fudging" the bottom line to avoid taxes. Sal immediately went to the president of his firm and was stunned to hear his reply: "Well, I am sure we can remedy this; he's one of our biggest clients you know. I am sure it will only take a minor adjustment, so you can sign off." Sal could hardly believe what he had heard.

After stewing for two days, Sal returned to his president and put his job on the line. "There are some lines I will not and cannot cross. I will resign before signing this tax statement," he said. This time, the president was stunned. He blushed and said, "You will not leave; we will do what is ethical here. And, by the way, thank you."

Just for today, I will ask myself where I would draw the line. I will commit to staying true to what I value.

"Take care of your body with steadfast fidelity. The soul must see through these eyes alone, and if they are dim, the whole world is clouded."

—Johann Wolfgang von Goethe

Are you aware of how your health affects your work? Anita was not. Anita was smart, emotionally in touch, and a real value to others. She had a high-stress job and always found reasons not to exercise, even though her office overlooked a large lake with a walking path. In her younger years, she laughed at people who exercised; because she did not have a weight problem, she thought she didn't need to work out. Anita had not realized how smug she had felt; she believed she was exempt from tending to her physical health.

When Anita had a heart attack at age forty-four, she got a wake-up call. Terror filled her; she came from a family with high rates of heart disease. She realized that she could no longer enjoy gourmet pizzas for lunch or rich cheeses at the day's end. Suddenly, Anita made room in her life for her health. She realized that a good heart and mind also needs health to sustain it. Anita now encourages others to join her in community fund-raising runs.

Just for today, I will pay attention to my health and recognize that my health is key to my overall success in my work and in other areas of my life.

"We're given a code to live our lives by. We don't always follow it, but it's still there."

—Gary Oldman

D o you follow a code of conduct? All too often, companies discover that they need a code of conduct *after the fact*—that is, after some behavioral violation has occurred.

Art and Joyce felt comfortable with their employees in their small family-owned business. Through the years, their work culture had always been respectful, so they were very surprised when some employees came to them with complaints that some of the managers were behaving disrespectfully. The employees reported being sent off-color jokes in their e-mails and receiving inappropriate "friendly" touches. Art and Joyce called an all-employee meeting and cited what they had learned. They then asked their employees to break into small groups and develop a code of conduct for their work environment. Joyce and Art, as well as all the employees, agreed to live their workdays by the resulting code of conduct; they all signed off on it. The employees once again felt secure with the company's strong leadership.

Just for today, I will ask myself what code of conduct I live by. I will model that behavior throughout my day, in and out of work.

August 20 ～ *Emotional Intelligence*

"When people go to work, they shouldn't have to leave their hearts at home."

—Betty Bender

Have you heard the term *emotional intelligence (EQ)?* Psychologist Daniel Goleman defines it as "the capacity for recognizing our own feelings and those of others, for motivating ourselves, and for managing emotions well in ourselves and in our relationships." In the late 1990s a large study showed that four out of five companies were trying to train employees in emotional intelligence.

When Larissa began a job that involved supervising hundreds of employees, she quickly saw EQ problems. The brilliant scientists on the staff seemed to have little awareness of their own feelings or those of others; they had created a culture that was cool and distanced. Larissa approached the problem by starting at the top; she asked her high-level employees to take EQ inventories. The inventory results indicated skills that needed further development. The scientists began a weekly seminar to develop their EQ, and within ten months, Larissa reported that the change was "palpable."

Just for today, I will evaluate my own emotional intelligence and try to identify areas that need development.

"Things are only worth what you make them worth."

—Molière

Just what is intellectual capital? Ruth learned the hard way about her intellectual capital. Over the years, she had developed a solid curriculum on financial planning; it was the core of her business. Ruth generously shared her knowledge at professional conferences. She had said, "Well, there are no original ideas, after all." One day, one of Ruth's former clients gave her a set of materials that was almost identical to her curriculum. Ruth was shocked. She had expected her professional colleagues to have the same ethics as she did. Ruth now reflected on the many years she had spent creating this curriculum—the time and energy she had invested in its research and development. She now truly understood what "intellectual capital" meant; she also recognized that, like financial capital, it could be stolen.

Ruth's partners wanted her to sue, but she firmly refused. She trusted that the curriculum was just as valuable, despite who presented it. Furthermore, she did not want to invest in the negative energy of a legal suit. She went on to create a new curriculum, and after copyrighting it, sold it to a financial planning firm.

Just for today, I will search my mind for my own intellectual capital. Just as important, I will recognize and honor the intellectual capital of others.

"During my eighty-seven years, I have witnessed a whole succession of technological revolutions. But none of them has done away with the need for character in the individual or the ability to think."

—Bernard M. Baruch

How does technology affect your life? What price do we pay for the benefits of this high technology? Today's technology affects our expectations; we seek immediacy in everything. We do not want any delayed gratification. We also see people leaving their families and loved ones to go on-line for hours. Sometimes we feel strangers are invading our living rooms, bedrooms, and offices with their commercial messages.

Recently, at a corporate meeting, two employees sent instant e-mail messages to each other rather than crossing the room to have a conversation. Their boss saw this and realized he had to set some limits. He approached them and teasingly, yet seriously, said, "Okay, guys, turn in your equipment." The same executive, with the help of his senior team, also developed a protocol for e-mail etiquette in the office.

Just for today, I will reflect on how I allow technology to control my life. I will consider what price I am paying for the immediacy in my work world.

"You can't outrun a guilty conscience."

—Sandra Brown

How do you see conscientiousness at work? Being conscientious means listening to the little voice within us that is our moral compass. Often we are tempted to take the "low road," but our conscience advises otherwise.

Roger had such an experience. He ran a very successful, high-cost, adventure travel company. He required a substantial nonrefundable deposit from his customers when they signed up for his trips; this allowed him to hire foreign guides in advance. All customers signed a waiver forfeiting their deposits if they cancelled within thirty days of the trip—*no matter what the reason.*

Roger had just received word that his expenses for an upcoming South American trip had increased due to conflicts in the region and necessary rerouting. One more customer would have covered the difference. Then Roger got the call. A woman had to cancel because her husband had become ill; she asked for a refund on her deposit since her husband was going to be out of work for a long time. Roger stewed; his policy was his policy. He felt torn because he was on a tight margin. Within a day, however, his conscience directed him; he refunded the money.

Just for today, I will listen to my conscience and be grateful that I possess such a strong moral compass.

August 24 ～ *Work as a Means to an End*

"Making a success of the job at hand is the best step toward the kind of life you want."

—Bernard M. Baruch

Do you know people who work as a means to an end? Often in self-help and spirituality books, work is discussed in lofty language—as being filled with purpose and meaning. This is not true for everyone, however. Some people work as a means to an end and keep it that simple.

Randy realized that building boats was his real passion and that living in the Southwest he could not earn a decent living in boat building. Since Randy needed free time to work on his boat, he wanted to work independently. He found a job as a manufacturer's representative in the women's clothing industry; this position allowed him to earn a high income for reasonable hours of work—and it left him enough time to pursue his passion. Friends and family wondered why he did not "fulfill" himself and use his ingenuity. But he *was* using his ingenuity. He just was not following the formula that so many of his peers had used. Randy would not have traded his passion for any nine-to-five job; he followed his heart.

Just for today, I will accept that it is not my responsibility to judge another's job. What matters is the quality of life we choose and are able to live.

"It is only as we develop others that we permanently succeed."

—Harvey S. Firestone

Have you ever noticed how satisfying it is to be involved in developing others?

For some time, Stewart, a vice president, felt he had been successful in developing others. When he went through a leadership assessment profile, however, he was surprised to receive low scores. In talking at length with Rick, a strong "developer" friend, Stewart learned that what he had been doing was micromanaging. He did not focus on people's strengths; rather, he pointed out problems and even found the solutions for them instead of letting them figure out their own solutions.

Stewart knew he needed help; Rick agreed to help him. Stewart was a quick learner; he identified what he called his "high potentials" and became a strong coach. He worked on his empathy skills and gave tips for performance increases. The best managers at the vice-presidential level or above focus on coaching their top employees. As Stewart developed his coaching skills, his employees, who admitted that they previously had gone outside for the help they needed, became much more successful.

Just for today, I will focus on how well I help others develop and what skills I might need to learn in order to foster growth in others.

August 26 ～ *Influence*

"Blessed is the influence of one true, loving human soul on another."

—George Eliot

Are you aware of how you influence others—and how others influence you? Our feelings and our moods affect those around us. In order to be successful in our work, we need to understand how influence works.

Recently, when arriving late in a city on a business trip, I arranged to take the shuttle to my hotel, which was located about eight miles from the airport. When the shuttle van finally arrived, the driver did a slow-down, not a real stop, and left without me. I ended up taking a taxi, arriving even later than expected. I was tired and my tone was quite indignant when I checked in at the front desk. The clerk listened carefully, made some notes, and then said, "Please sign this; we will refund the seventeen-dollar taxi fare." He continued, "We are very sorry."

Suddenly, my weariness left me; this kind, attentive act truly influenced my mood. The hotel clerk had taken the first step in using influence; he had built rapport. This simple example reminded me of how easily we can influence others.

Just for today, I will be mindful of how I use my influence and how others can influence me. I will focus on rapport building.

"If you don't make things happen, then things will happen to you."

—Lanes Company

Can you recall an event you helped effect because of your initiative? When people have initiative, they can foresee something fresh; they do not have to wait for an external stimulus to act.

Lorraine could see that her not-for-profit organization was struggling to win research grants because of their new area of technology. The organization's computer specialists were working in informatics, a new field, and came from academic environments where other people were responsible for writing grants. Raising money held no appeal to the computer specialists; they said they had not come there to do fund-raising.

Lorraine knew she had to do something. After talking to others at professional conferences, she decided to form a small grant-writing department where grant writers could work closely with the computer specialists. The board supported her initiative to hire three grant writers; and shortly thereafter, large grants were secured. Lorraine's initiative became a win-win situation.

Just for today, I will explore what opportunities I might seize, I will use my optimism to move matters forward.

August 28 ⟋ *Organizational Intelligence*

"I not only use all the brains I have, but all the brains that I can borrow."

—Woodrow Wilson

Do you have a sense of your company's organizational intelligence? *Organizational intelligence* refers to an organization's capacity for problem solving, for meeting challenges, and for creating or revising products. When knowledge and competence are spread throughout an organization, we see organizational intelligence.

Fern's workplace had always worked with a "silo" structure. Different work groups were separated, and they seldom gathered together. She knew that they had remarkably bright people throughout the company, but they never seemed to be able to put their energies together for the good of the whole. Fern decided to restructure, and when she did the silos tumbled. Now the groups were multidisciplinary and were able to help one another with problem solving. They quickly found that what they thought was a problem in one area was easily resolved when viewed by an employee from a different discipline. Fern smiled when she saw the high energy as the new teams worked together. They truly had collapsed their individual intelligence into organizational intelligence.

Just for today, I will examine my own contribution to my company's organizational intelligence.

"We are enslaved by anything we do not consciously see. We are freed by conscious perception."

—Vernon Howard

Is your performance measured? If so, by what? Today, we see the area of performance measures changing dramatically.

When the owners of a small greeting card company came together to assess their performance, they decided that their current feedback instruments were not enough. They resolved to assess one another—as a team and with honesty. Traditionally they had measured their individual performances by reviewing the revenue they each produced. When they began analyzing their performances by identifying their contributions, however, they found the unexpected.

Linda would never have gained three major customers without the introductions and setups she received from two of the other owners who had strong community ties. They also learned that the revenue stream was likely sustained through one of the owners' ongoing visits with the small businesses; this owner was an expert in small business operations. These examples showed the owners that they truly needed to be evaluated by their greatest strength—their contribution to the team. They had now made the transition to measuring themselves as a team.

Just for today, I will ask myself how my performance is measured. What measures do I use to assess my own performance and growth?

August 30 ～ *Revealing Yourself*

"Integrity simply means a willingness not to violate one's identity."

—Erich Fromm

How do you choose to reveal yourself to others with whom you work? How much do you want your co-workers to know about you?

Timothy was the head of his division in a large health management system. The environment there was quite friendly and the mission statement included words of "an inclusive environment." When the holiday season approached during Timothy's second year at the company, he decided to hold an open house for his employees. What his colleagues did not know, however, was that Timothy was in a long-term, committed relationship—with a man. His partner offered to leave the house when Timothy entertained, but Timothy said, "No, you won't. This is who we are and this is who their boss is."

Timothy knew that when his colleagues toured his old Victorian condominium, they would see it was a one-bedroom unit. The evening went smoothly; as a result of Timothy's willingness to be open about his life, two employees came forth to reveal their gayness to Timothy. He had led the way in revealing himself.

Just for today, I will be sensitive to what might not be revealed to me by others. I will also ask myself how comfortable I am with revealing myself to my colleagues.

"There is never a better measure of what a person is than what he does when he is absolutely free to choose."

—William M. Bulger

Just what do we mean by *self-mastery*? Does the term ring true for you? Self-mastery means knowing what your limitations are and what brings you the deepest satisfaction.

While Bill was in a leadership role, those in his inner circle knew that he was neither a strong leader nor a strong manager. Highly intelligent, he had mastered his area of science. Yet, entering a new position in a burgeoning industry, he was stressed and unaware of how the high stress affected his behavior. He relied heavily on the logic that he had been trained in. Anything outside logical thinking he termed "the touchy-feely stuff."

Bill had had no training in affective education, or feeling education. During Bill's annual review, he recognized that his self-mastery was wavering. It was outdated. With feedback, he recognized his limitations. Although he had considered early retirement, he ultimately decided to stay and focus on the hard stuff—the soft side—of his business. He started the process of self-assessment and development of his intuitive skills.

Just for today, I will ask myself if I understand my own self-mastery. I will assess my use of my "inner rudder."

September

Gifts ⌣ September 1

"The question is not 'Do I have the gifts and strengths that I need for my life, but am I seeking to discover my gifts and strengths?'"

—Paula Ripple

Do you know what your gifts are? A gift is something you are given; you don't have to earn it or work at it. Richard Leider, coauthor of *Whistle While You Work,* emphasizes that our talents, our natural gifts, are a blessing from beyond and require no theological perspective. It's often easier to identify the gifts others have than it is to realize our own gifts. To discover our gifts, we can ask ourselves, "What am I naturally good at?" If we don't hear an answer, we can ask someone close to us. Our gifts could be activities, such as facilitating meetings, or the ability to easily learn languages or play music.

Maria, a native of Cuba, had a natural gift for playing the guitar and singing. She loved to sing Spanish songs from her childhood. Unfortunately, she saw no place at work for using this gift. When she learned that many of the employees who worked in the company cafeteria were people of Mexican descent, she offered to perform for them in Spanish at the end of lunchtime, to share her gifts with others. Groups gathered daily, from inside and outside the cafeteria, and employees returned to work with lifted spirits.

Just for today, I will reflect on what my gifts are and consider how I can incorporate them into my work.

September 2 ⌒ *Right Brain, Left Brain*

"Whenever I have heavy problems I simply introduce the question to my mind, what the problem is, and, in time, I always get an answer."

—James M. Benham

The two sides of the brain perform different functions. The left side controls the right side of the body and mainly deals with language, time, and logic. The right side, which controls the left side of the body, mainly deals with vision, intuition, and spatial orientation. Scientists and psychologists have found that we are most creative when the right and left sides of the brain work together—when we practice what's known as whole-brain management.

A business group that was working with some corporate trainers became quite suspicious about some of the whole-brain-management exercises they were asked to do. As they integrated such concepts as intuition and nonverbal readings through experiential exercises, however, they began to have fun. It did not take long for them to learn that these new techniques expanded their business creativity and led to bottom-line increases. The group spread the training message throughout their organization.

Just for today, I will consider how I am bringing my whole self, my whole brain, into my work—alone and with others.

"Coming together is a beginning, staying together is progress, and working together is success."

—Henry Ford

How would you describe the management in your workplace? Is it top-down management, or is it people-oriented, "working with," management?

After attending a month-long seminar on management styles, Daniel decided to change his management style. He knew it would be difficult at first. He had inherited the business from his father, who led with a demeaning style. Daniel had to face issues of trust as he formed self-management teams. At first, the self-managed work teams did not know how to work together; they had to learn to trust themselves and their decision making. Along the way, some employees left; they could not adjust to the new, more democratic management in the firm. Those who stayed, however, soon became more satisfied and productive than ever before.

Just for today, I will allow my own management style to be as egalitarian as possible.

September 4 ～ *Family Businesses*

"When they are working well, families can bring a level of commitment, long-range investment, rapid action, and love for the company that nonfamily businesses yearn for but seldom achieve."

—Kelin Gersick

Do you work in a family-owned business? Between 65 and 80 percent of businesses are family firms—from the corner grocery store to Wal-Mart. The challenge for owners of family businesses is to learn how to live and work in two subsystems—the family and the business.

Sally had been named CEO of her four-generation family business and felt confident in her role. However, Sally's younger sister, Susan, deeply resented Sally's leadership and often tried to form a triangle by calling in their brother, Josh, to settle conflicts. The family was not comfortable with expressing feelings, and the buried feelings created tension. Finally, exhausted from the energy it took to work with her siblings, Sally decided to bring in a consultant. As the family told their history, the siblings discovered that directly under the business system were unresolved childhood resentments. As forgiveness and understanding surfaced, the business and the family systems flourished; the caring in the family was vital and visible.

Just for today, I will recognize that my family feelings accompany me into my workplace. I will ask myself if I have any unfinished "family business."

"Your own safety is at stake when your neighbor's wall is ablaze."

—Horace

How safe do you feel at work physically? Today we often read about companies sponsoring self-protection and safety workshops because employees do not feel safe. Workplace violence is on the rise; more than forty workplace shootings have occurred since 1980. Our physical safety is also at risk when workers are tired or discouraged, or have poor working conditions. Another type of safety that affects our well-being is emotional safety. How safe do you feel at work emotionally? Are feelings to be checked at the door?

Harry's company decided to improve its work culture. It introduced models of conflict resolution and encouraged employees to express their feelings. Not only did the work environment begin to feel more comfortable, but the accident rate on the factory floor was soon cut in half! The plant managers began to see the connection between emotional and physical safety.

Just for today, I will conduct myself in ways that create a safe environment for those around me as well as for myself.

September 6 ～ *Glass Ceiling*

"An occupation that has no basis in sex-determined gifts can now recruit its ranks from twice as many potential artists."

—Margaret Mead

Is there a glass ceiling where you work? Have you considered that what's glass might not be the ceiling at all, but rather the foundation, the walls, and the air you breathe? Three approaches are typically used in rationalizing gender discrimination. They all assume that women don't "fit"; this surely affects the spirits of women at work.

To illustrate the approaches, imagine a group of tall people in a short world. What if the power people were all under 5'5"? In the first approach, the tall people call for change, saying, "We can fit!" (women assimilate by wearing men's clothes and playing golf). In the second approach, some short people tell the tall people that they can fix the structural barrier and make higher doors and desks (accommodation through flex time and maternity leaves). The third approach would be to celebrate differences by praising tallness and rewarding it (women head human resources departments and market to women).

All three approaches are symptom removal; they do not address the real problem. When women have equality, both men and women will win, and we can be more spiritually whole.

Just for today, I will be aware of what I tell myself about a glass ceiling. I will be mindful about the humanness shared by women and men and how discrimination flattens the spirit.

"No culture can live if it attempts to be exclusive."

—Mahatma Gandhi

How much cultural diversity exists in your workplace? Do you work among people of diverse color, ethnicity, race, and gender? While our differences enrich all of our lives, it takes time to work through our cultural stereotypes.

Shawn was asked to lead a cross-cultural seminar in which a team of physicians from Russia and the United States would discuss cultural differences that could surface in their joint endeavor. Shawn had the two groups face one another. He asked the Americans to state what they believed the Russian people thought of them. They used words such as *capitalistic, individualistic,* and *imperialistic.* Simply put, they owned their own stereotypes, and the Russians heartily laughed at what they heard. They had indeed named the Russian stereotypes of them. Shawn then reversed the exercise and the Russians used words such as *communist, atheistic,* and *rigid.* As the groups named their own cultural stereotypes in front of each other, they removed some of the hidden tension. This put them in a healthy place, a point from which they could start to bridge the cultural differences they would ultimately face.

Just for today, I will assess the cultural diversity in my own world, both in and out of work, and recognize the similarities among all people.

September 8 ～ Type A

"On the brink of a new stage of human development, we are racing blindly into the future. But where do we want to go?"

—Alvin Toffler

What do you know about type A behavior? Have you ever been told that you have a type A personality? Dr. Meyer Friedman, a cardiologist who first identified type A behavior, came upon it by observing patients who were wearing down the upholstery on his waiting-room furniture. The people fidgeted so much that they wore the fabric through. In observing further, he discovered that these people also rushed everywhere, were irritable, and were often angry or rageful.

Type A behavior has become more common; the rage is also spreading. Dr. Friedman realized that he was a member of this group, and he worked hard to change the patterns of his stress-filled life. Today, researchers teach type A people to ask themselves this question before they act: "Will this matter five years from now?" Of course, the answer is usually no. When we slow down, we experience more.

Just for today, I will ask myself how much time I will save if I rush. I will acknowledge that I have all the time I need.

Quitting ⌒ September 9

"When we walk to the edge of all the light we have to take the step into the darkness of the unknown, and we must believe that one of two things will happen. There will be something solid for us to stand on or we will be taught to fly."

—Patrick Overton

Have you ever quit a job? At times, such a move is quite appropriate.

Because of the amount of travel required for Leonard's job, he seldom saw his four-year-old son or his wife. At one point, he felt that his relationship with his wife was becoming distanced. On a long flight back from Europe one day, he decided that he had to quit. Leonard's wife, Nancy, supported him in his decision. He began looking for jobs with less travel, but he also wanted to take his time and choose well. When his boss asked him to go on another four-week trip, Leonard trusted his instincts and resigned, on the spot, without the security of having another position lined up. Within two months, Leonard realized that quitting had been the right decision; he was grateful for his trust. During this time he did find a new job.

Just for today, I will ask myself whether my work sustains me.

September 10 ～ *Emotional Awareness*

"Cherish your own emotions and never undervalue them."

—Robert Henri

Emotional awareness is the ability to identify when you're experiencing a feeling and then to allow yourself to feel it. Emotions can drive our behavior at work, so awareness of our emotions can be essential to our competency at work.

When Robin learned that her senior team partners wanted to restructure the company, she resisted. She told Bert, a team member and friend, that she did not see a need for change. She rigidly opposed all the options on the table. Bert finally asked her what she was afraid of. Robin denied any fear, but Bert saw through her. When Bert softly told Robin it was okay to be afraid, tears ran down Robin's cheeks. Bert was the catalyst, helping Robin become aware of her emotions regarding the restructuring. With this information, Robin could begin exploring her fears and then join the discussion.

Just for today, I will focus on how aware I am of my emotions. When I have strong feelings, I will try to name them.

Cheating ⟋ September 11

"Oh, what wondrous webs we weave—when at first we do deceive."

—William Shakespeare

Have you ever wanted to cheat at work? Perhaps they were "little cheats"—misrepresenting financials or withholding some information.

Matt's work group was excited about their half-day outing to a nearby rock-climbing site. They had agreed to two purposes—self-awareness and team building. When Matt became stuck while climbing up the rock face, he moved far over to the left of the rope, off of the "climbing route." The consultants warned him of the dangers—that he could swing and scrape himself. Yet Matt continued to move over and desperately grabbed a tree trunk that grew out of the corner of the rocks. Far off his route, he saw that the only way out was to swing and risk hurting himself. "Where else are you cheating in your life, Matt?" asked the instructor. Matt froze; his body had not lied. Indeed, he had been deceptive in creating his regional sales reports. During the group discussion later, Matt admitted his fudging to the group and realized how ashamed he felt with his secret.

Just for today, I will be aware of any temptations to cheat and recognize that deceptions will take me off my life climb.

September 12 ⌒ *Narcissism*

"A person wrapped up in himself makes a small package."

—Harry Emerson Fosdick

Have you ever worked with or for a narcissist? Narcissists often hold strong leadership positions; they are concerned with image and always want to appear to be doing the "right thing." Their self-centeredness usually results in a lot of ego-driven behavior and "I" language.

When Ted accepted a new position on Wall Street, he was very excited. After a few months on the job, however, he realized that his boss was narcissistic. His boss did not want anyone to outshine him. When Ted read a magazine article on narcissistic leaders, he realized what he was dealing with. In time, Ted chose to leave. His wife asked him whether he had looked at how he was fooled—how had he become snared into the narcissism. Ted paused and said, "I think he enticed my ego; he kept flattering me—telling me how special I was." Ted realized how his ego was vulnerable to the cunning of the narcissist; he was grateful for this lesson.

Just for today, I will observe what actions can entice my ego; I know that my ego is vulnerable. Staying in touch with my spirit will protect my balance.

> *"Enjoying success requires the ability to adapt. Only by being open to change will you have a true opportunity to get the most from your talent."*
>
> —Nolan Ryan

Have you ever had to relocate for your job? How well was your move handled?

Anita had painful memories of how her relocation was handled in her first job. Sent to a site in Asia, she had received no cultural preparation or language training. She recalled spending long hours standing in line to register for all services, often to find it was the wrong line. She needed to search for housing while being responsible for a start-up business. She also needed to learn a new business climate and meet prospective clients. Anita succeeded because she was willing to learn and adapt. She took time daily to breathe, meditate, and read meditations. When it was time for Anita to relocate other employees, she was confident in what they needed. She arranged for informal meetings with cultural specialists, made arrangements with a housing relocation agency, and had local people help the employees get settled. The employees were very grateful for Anita's assistance.

Just for today, I will ask myself what I do when I have to make any changes in my work system and how I prepare for any changes through nurturing my spirit.

September 14 ⌒ *Exclusion*

"Care is the state in which something does matter: it is the source of human tenderness."

—Rollo May

Have you ever felt excluded at work? Sometimes we can feel excluded from a particular group or project. Temporary workers often report feeling excluded.

Terry had indeed noticed the new group of employees who had come through the training program. She was cordial but with her busy schedule, she did not want to share any of her free time with strangers. She had many good friends she had grown up with in the company. One day the human resources director called Terry and her friend Diane into her office. "I need you both," she began. "I know you don't intend to exclude people, but I want you to ask yourselves if you have ever felt excluded and what that was like for you. Our new employees are struggling to belong, and they don't think you are making it easy for them," she said thoughtfully. After Terry and Diane reflected on their own times of exclusion, they both made the commitment to open their circle to the new employees. Inclusion can cultivate a sense of total well-being in an organization.

Just for today, I will examine whether anyone seems to be excluded. Knowing the loneliness of exclusion, I will reach out to that person.

"There is no place you can go and only be with people who are like you. Give it up."

—Bernice Johnson Reagon

Have you ever noticed how ethnicity affects the climate in your workplace? Often the ethnic backgrounds of the people at the top of an organization shape the rules by which the organization will be governed. Is yours a high-touch, warm, outgoing system? Or is it aloof, distanced, and low touch? While we can tease about ethnic differences and stereotypes, there are some generalities.

Georgio, a native of Italy, liked to stand very close to other people. When Jeanette, a Norwegian, had to interact with him, she often felt uncomfortable; she felt invaded. In the same firm, Adela, who is Hispanic, felt very comfortable with her small outbursts that seemed to pass quickly. Realizing that ethnicity factors were contributing both negatively and positively to the organization, Lucille set up an ethnic diversity day for the entire office staff. With humor, cartoon slides, and personal stories of their ethnic histories, the employees left the seminar with a new appreciation for their ethnic differences.

Just for today, I will remind myself that we all have ethnic roots; no one is excluded. I will focus on respecting ethnic differences and not judging others.

September 16 ~ Scapegoats

"To err is human; to blame the next guy even more so."

—Unknown

Is there a perennial scapegoat in your work world? Often what the scapegoat does not ask is, "How did I accept the invitation?" When a workplace has unfinished business—that is, the company has not dealt with some of its own negative "baggage" from the past—the system creates an opening for a scapegoat.

Phyllis seemed to become the scapegoat wherever she worked. She did not recognize what part she played in creating her role. When a friend confronted her about being in the fourth job in which she was the scapegoat, she decided to examine her history. She was tired of being blamed and being the recipient of the negative attitudes in the system. The next time her company looked for a scapegoat for a new problem, she refused the invitation to the role by standing up for herself. She said that although her views were different, she would cooperate and contribute to work projects. In this case, the entire system didn't have to change—just Phyllis.

Just for today, I will be alert to the elements at play to create a scapegoat. I will not engage in creating a scapegoat.

"I am only one; but still I am one. I cannot do everything, but still I can do something; I will not refuse to do something I can do."

—Helen Keller

Stewardship means appreciating and upholding the historic values of your company or organization. As a "good" steward, you may feel like a guardian of a workplace legacy that has been passed on to you.

Milton had a deep appreciation for his company's legacy of honoring its employees. He was a courageous steward and held fast to the original intent of the founding family members. As Milton neared retirement, he thought about the business values that had been carefully passed down through four generations. Having worked with two of the four generations, Milton wanted to contribute to the stewardship philosophy. He hired a corporate history writer to record his company's history. The writer, after interviewing almost one hundred people, was struck by the loyalty, the sense of appreciation, and sense of family that was alive in the organization. Milton recognized that his contribution would add just one other piece to the stewardship philosophy.

Just for today, I will ask myself where I experience stewardship in my life. I will also ask myself what I can contribute to guiding principles in my work life.

September 18 ～ *Inadequacy*

"You gain strength, courage, and confidence by every experience in which you really stop to look fear in the face."

—Eleanor Roosevelt

Just where and how do you experience feelings of inadequacy? Is it in the written word, in speaking, or in creating ideas? We may feel competent in many areas of our lives yet fear pockets of inadequacy.

Allan had worked for many years with the same work group, who often complained about Allan's refusal to provide written summaries of his work. They were not sure whether it was procrastination or outright refusal. When a consultant suggested that Allan write a book about the group's unique work environment, Allan was filled with fear. Casually, the nonsuspecting consultant said, "Well, when will the work begin?" Allan then confessed, "I cannot write; I haven't written since sixth grade! And I feel very ashamed of that." The consultant challenged Allan about his old beliefs and sent him to a writing seminar. Within months, Allan told his work group about his fear and he grew in self-confidence while he healed his shame.

Just for today, I will ask myself in what context I feel inadequate and how I might work through it.

"It's good to shut up sometimes."

—Marcel Marceau

Have you ever worked with someone who crossed the line of professionalism? When someone crosses the line, our relationship with that person can totally change.

When Freida called Jim, her financial planner, she could hear strain in his voice. She empathetically said that perhaps she should call back later. At this point, Jim began telling Freida what was going on in his personal life. He talked about his pending divorce and child custody suit. Freida was shocked; they had always had a highly professional relationship; now Jim was crossing the line into the personal arena. Since Freida entrusted Jim with her personal savings, she was uncomfortable hearing about his personal problems that might interfere with his work. And when Jim tearfully told her that he no longer trusted his business decisions, Freida felt that he had definitely crossed a line. Although she sympathized with what Jim was going through, she felt that his extensive disclosure had irrevocably damaged their client-consultant relationship. For Freida, it was important to keep her business relationships at a professional level.

Just for today, I will pay attention to the personal and professional boundary line. I will carefully consider whom I share my personal life with.

September 20 ～ Satisfaction

"Far and away the best prize that life offers is the chance to work hard at work worth doing."

—Theodore Roosevelt

What parts of your job bring you satisfaction? If you rated your satisfaction at work on a ten-point scale, with ten being high, what score you would give yourself?

Andrea worked in a medical office; her job was to greet patients and make certain that their records were ready for the physicians. One day she was visiting with friends when they all decided to rate their job satisfaction. Andrea was pleasantly surprised that she rated her satisfaction as eight. Her friends asked how her job, which entailed "waiting on others," could possibly be satisfying. Andrea replied assuredly and warmly that being of service to both the outer office (the patients) and the inner office (the physicians she worked for) gave her deep satisfaction. "I consider my job to provide good service all the way 'round," she said. Andrea explained that her spirit felt at peace at work; her friends realized that to be true of Andrea.

Just for today, I will ask myself what brings me satisfaction in my work and what changes I may need to make, if any, to become more satisfied.

"Men, for the sake of getting a living, forget to live."

—Margaret Fuller

Rejuvenation is important for all of us. Just how do you become renewed or rejuvenated in your work life? While it is surely satisfying to simply leave work and take an extended holiday, that's not always possible. Yet we can find other ways to breathe freshness into our workday so that we can approach it with renewed, restored spirits.

Nancy decided that she needed to interrupt her routine in order to rejuvenate herself. She envied her two friends who were able to walk to work. Nancy found a simple solution. She began parking her car almost two miles from work and walking to her office. On her walks, she paid particular attention to her surroundings. One morning she did a "window" walk, focusing on all the different windows she walked by, then a "chimney walk," a "shrub walk," and so on. When Nancy arrived at work, she found she approached her day with a restored spirit. She also made an effort to get to know more people in her workplace, from employees in the cafeteria to the mailroom. Through these simple acts, Nancy restored her spirit.

Just for today, I will ask myself how I can rejuvenate myself at work.

"Most people see what they want to, or at least what they expect to."

—Martha Grimes

How rigid are your perspectives at work? Sometimes it is hard to detach ourselves from the glue holding our perspectives.

Recently, I worked with a group of executives whose thinking did not fit with the entrepreneurial company. They were stuck in an old linear model, one they had learned years ago while attending business school. One of the younger members in the group challenged the others' assumptions and urged them to think "outside the box." Upon self-reflection, the group members were quite surprised at how attached they had become to the security of their long-standing perspectives. When they admitted it was time to face their fears of letting go of control and security, they were able to brainstorm and create new possibilities for an upcoming reorganization. They also realized that if they were to continue building their entrepreneurial business, they had to be open to fresh perspectives. Through this experience, the executives saw the connection between fresh perspectives and lively spirits.

Just for today, I will examine how fresh my perspectives are. I will welcome the ideas of others to broaden my own perspectives.

"No matter how far you've gone down the wrong road, turn back."

—Turkish proverb

Awake-up call—a life-changing event or circumstance—can indeed be a gift. Sometimes wake-up calls are related to our work.

Hugh had worked long hours in his entrepreneurial firm. At forty-one, he was very successful financially and also rich in his family life, with three young daughters and a wife who was his best friend. He kept telling himself that within three years he could slow down; by then he would have met his goals. At his yearly physical, however, Hugh learned that he had cancer. He felt stunned as he drove home; he could not tell his wife, Janeen, until later that night when the children were asleep. Together, they cried. Hugh realized this was a wake-up call—the awakening crisis that bolted him into full awareness of what his life had been about in these start-up years. Hugh and Janeen immediately set goals for their next years and listed their priorities. Suddenly Hugh's business was no longer a top priority; his family was.

Just for today, I will ask myself how I can live most fully, without a wake-up call.

September 24 ⌒ *Newness*

"There are no new ideas. There are only new ways of making them felt."

—Audre Lorde

How do you experience newness in your work life? Is it through travel, implementing new ideas, changing how you approach tasks? Some people talk with friends in similar roles to learn how they bring newness into their work lives. Other people find newness automatically in their work—new clients, new patients, new students, for example. For still others, newness can be a challenge; it is not automatic and needs to be created.

We can keep our work lives fresh and new through small changes in our methods for our work roles and procedures; we do not need to make major changes. Some people report that finding newness outside of work allows them to bring their fresh attitudes into work. If we want newness in our lives, we cannot be passive about it; we must reach out to other people and experiences.

Just for today, I will ask myself what I am doing to bring newness into my work. Newness comes readily to an active spirit.

"Tender hearts as well were hearts of stone / If what they feel is for themselves alone."

—Jane Taylor

Do you witness sensitive acts at your workplace? Often we can see sensitivity in subtle, small ways.

As Dan prepared to chair a planning committee meeting, he noted that the retiring chair emeritus of the firm, eighty-nine-year-old Edward, had entered the meeting room. It was clear that Edward thought he belonged in the meeting. Dan had told the others that this was a closed meeting; they had important decisions to make. Edward took his place and sat attentively. Dan did not know quite what to do; he did not want to tell Edward to leave. He began, "Now since this is our first meeting, let me read the list of members who constitute this group so we can take a roll call." As Edward heard the list, he suddenly stood up. "Well, this is clear to me; I am in the wrong meeting," he said. "I apologize." Dan, through his sensitivity, preserved Edward's dignity.

Just for today, I will be sensitive to the feelings of everyone around me. I know that sensitivity is part of my spiritual connection to others.

September 26 ~ *Rituals*

"Rituals are the formulas by which harmony is restored."

—Terry Tempest Williams

Can you readily identify the rituals in your work-place? Through our rituals we experience stability and constancy in our work lives. We use rituals to formally recognize achievements, celebrate special occasions, mark transitions, or express our deepest beliefs.

Roberta decided to begin a "feeling connection" with her co-workers. During her group's regular Monday morning meeting, she asked each member to offer a brief personal check-in to the group. There were to be no comments or dialogue—just check-ins about what the members were feeling or what was going on in their lives. After a long pause, Roberta asked her co-workers to try it for just a month, and they agreed. Roberta modeled exactly what she wanted by stating how she felt and what was going on in her work and personal life. In time, the group members found that the ritual helped bring them closer together and, thus, improved their work relationships. They decided to continue their ritual.

Just for today, I will notice the rituals in my workplace. It may be up to me to create the safe space for people to bring their personhood to work.

"Deep change comes from real personal growth . . . through learning and unlearning."

—Peter Senge

Often, for our spiritual growth, we must unlearn old behaviors and beliefs.

Ron had learned from his father how to be discounting, sarcastic, and controlling. Just as people feared his father, Ron's workforce feared him. Then one day his wife walked out on their marriage, leaving him with three young children. Desperate, Ron turned to his minister. As he focused on his personal growth and uncovered feelings he had buried years ago, he began to explore how he conducted himself at work. When he asked his employees to complete a feedback survey, he felt despair at the findings. His employees described him as he had described his father—discounting and controlling. Ron had normalized his father's mean-spirited behavior, behavior Ron's father had learned from *his* father. Ron slowly began to change and find his true self—what he believed in, what mattered to him, and what he wanted to show his children. His behavior at work gradually revealed all his unlearning. In time, his children noticed a change, as did his workforce; Ron's spirit was coming to life.

Just for today, I will ask myself what I must unlearn and take a first step toward that change in my life.

September 28 ～ Denial

"If everybody lives roughly the same lies about the same things, there is no one to call them liars. They jointly establish their own sanity and call themselves normal."

—Ernest Becker

Many of us have witnessed denial at work. When we see denial, we see a group conforming to its own "normality."

Lou faced denial when he told his corporate counsel about questionable behavior that could result in a lawsuit. The incident he reported involved some fearful women who had been subjected to unwanted intimate touch at a company party. The offender was the president of the company. Within one week, Lou was called into the director of human resources office and told that he was to take a three-month leave of absence. No explanation came; Lou felt devastated. When he sought outside help, he learned about his own denial: he had not remembered that the counsel and president were best friends. When Lou did return to work, his office was no longer in the executive suite and he had a new job title. Fortunately, Lou was learning more about how his own denial fit perfectly into the denial at his office. As his denial began to break, Lou found the core of his spiritual growth; he resigned with dignity and reality intact.

Just for today, I will ask myself where I might experience denial in my own life. What do I not allow myself to see? I will take steps to learn what is real.

"Creativity often consists in merely turning up what is already there. Did you know that right and left shoes were thought up only a little more than a century ago?"

—Bernice Fitz-Gibbon

W hen people feel hopeful, they can re-vision what is possible and where they are going.

In a large urban hospital, the senior nursing staff had been working in a disrespectful environment for years. They felt hopeless to change the work vision, yet they stayed—committed to service and healing. When their hospital administrator retired early, they were relieved yet fearful that his replacement might also dupe the board of directors. When the new administrator started, he shocked the employees by asking for a three-hour meeting with each member of the senior staff. They were astonished. After their first team meeting, the group was excited; they had never experienced such a meeting with their previous administrator. The group gathered together to develop strategies that would help their new boss succeed at the hospital. Their new leader had given them an opportunity to revise their vision— they discovered a vision of spiritual hope.

Just for today, I will ask myself where and how I can revise my vision. I know that my vision keeps me spiritually alive.

September 30 ⌒ *Sexism*

"Sexism goes so deep that at first it's hard to see; you think it's just reality."

—Alix Kates Shulman

How do you respond when you see sexist behaviors? Melinda, a business consultant, was used to being treated respectfully. At a pre-retreat dinner with six businessmen who were merging their companies, however, she was shocked with what she saw. As the wine consumption increased, the businessmen began ogling the waitresses and some made near off-color comments. As their meeting opened the next morning, Melinda said, "I cannot go forward with you all until we have a discussion. I must let you know how offended I was last night with behaviors I saw. You see," she continued, "while I have always felt respected by you, I am a woman, and when you are disrespectful of my gender, I feel that I, too, am disrespected. And if I am to complete this work with you, I must see respect . . . of all." The group stared; there were moments of silence before the men responded apologetically. They showed their remorse, and Melinda agreed to go forward. Melinda completed her work, feeling respect—her own self-respect as well as theirs.

Just for today, I will ask myself how I will respond to sexism I witness. I will recognize that my spirit grows when I respect and feel respected.

October

"To say, 'Well done' to any bit of good work is to take hold of the powers which have made the effort and strengthen them beyond our knowledge."

—Phillip Brooks

Do you feel recognized at work? Maureen, an administrative assistant, spent fourteen years working for the same man and seldom received recognition for her contributions. When her boss left the company, Maureen was tentative about a new boss. "Will the new guy be different—will he see what I do?" she asked herself. When Ned, her new boss, arrived, he told Maureen that he wanted her to attend all team meetings. At her first meeting, Ned introduced Maureen and praised her years of service and her loyalty. He told the others that she would be included in all meetings from that day forward. As they were leaving the meeting, one of her co-workers asked, "How does it feel to finally be recognized for all you have contributed and to be treated with such respect?" Maureen felt tears rolling down her face and walked away, nodding. Ned knew recognition costs little—perhaps just a few seconds of time—touches the heart, and ignites the spirit.

Just for today, I will enjoy any special moments of recognition and know that while I can exist without it, recognition does nourish my spirit.

October 2 〜 Silos

"We're all in this alone."

—Lily Tomlin

Silos are singular structures, standing tall and alone. Self-contained, they are not dependent on any connection to have a place. Silos exist in workplaces, too, and some people work in silos without recognizing it.

In a corporate training seminar, I conducted a "silo exercise," asking people to move around the room as though they were silos. The participants kept their distances, moving toward others and then backing away. They kept to their own spaces and ignored the other silos. At the end of the exercise, the participants described how they felt during silo experience—they reported feeling disconnected and lonely and said they lacked empathy for the needs of others. Next, they considered how their behavior during the exercise corresponded to how they conducted themselves at work. The participants concluded that acting as a silo in the workplace was bad not only for the company but also for the spirit. The group of employees made a commitment to change their metaphor from a silo to a tapestry. They discussed what a tapestry would need—interweaving, closeness, creativity, color. What better metaphor for creating a spiritually friendly workplace?

Just for today, I will ask myself how and when I experience the "silo." What will I have to give up in order to become part of a tapestry? What will I gain through this transformation?

"It is a curious fact that the more ignorant and degraded a man is, the more contemptuously he holds those whom he deems inferior."

—Joseph Conrad

Do you experience racism in your workplace? How do you react to it?

Aymee was honored when she was invited to a company dinner with visiting international dignitaries. When she entered the corporate dining room, she sat between one of the dignitaries and her boss. Directly across from her sat the executive vice president. Aymee, nervous, focused on her breathing to stay grounded. Then, out of nowhere, the executive across from her made a racist comment, intending it to be humorous. Aymee was stunned; she knew she could not be silent. Aymee turned her eyes to the ceiling and said aloud, "Dear God, I cannot believe I just heard what I heard at this table!" The executive immediately offered a limp excuse, at which point Aymee looked upward again and said, "Then, why, dear God, did he say it in the first place?" Satisfied that she'd acknowledged and dealt with the situation the best way she could, she resumed conversation with those around her. She did not forfeit her integrity to protect someone; this was a spiritual pledge.

Just for today, I will ask myself how I respond to racism, overtly or covertly, in my work systems.

October 4 ～ *Cultural Constraints*

"Cultural constraints condition and limit our choices, shaping our character with their imperatives."

—Jean Fitzpatrick

Are there constraints in your company culture? Tim worked at a company that had enjoyed great economic success. The workplace itself was also pleasant to look at, with an abundance of lovely plants and rich wood furniture. Yet, despite the trappings, Tim knew the company was spiritually impoverished. People were so politely formal that no one really knew one another, and the constraints of this company culture led Tim to consider leaving his job. At an all-company party one night, Tim decided to break the superficiality rule. Talking with the vice president, he said, "You know, this is one of the most boring and polite workplaces I have ever seen in my life. Do you think it will ever change?" The vice president flushed; surrounding people were silent. Tim left the party early, very worried. The next morning, several of his co-workers approached Tim and thanked him for speaking his truth. "You spoke for a bunch of us. How can we thank you?" they said. Another bonus came when the vice president called him in and praised him for "naming" the problem so clearly. This was the firm's first step in its spiritual journey.

Just for today, I will identify any cultural constraints I face that block my spiritual growth. I will take action for my spirit.

"When we stand up in the center, we find the stillpoint within."

—Barbara Shipka

When was the last time that you were drawn, like a magnet, away from the center of your own world? All of us are vulnerable to being pulled away from our own inner knowing. Recently I called my colleague and friend Barbara and asked her for a consultation regarding my lack of progress with a corporate client. Barbara helped me understand that I was letting their "stuckness" take me away from my own truth. She gently and wisely reminded me that I was taking their fear-driven process personally. She then used the example of standing like an upright paper clip in the center of a tile, with magnetic borders surrounding the tile. These magnets represent all those life forces that can impact us and draw us away from our center. "Our task," she reminded me, "is to keep ourselves upright and within our center." Barbara's metaphor helped me recognize just what had happened. In connecting with the metaphor, I could feel myself taking my own power back (straightening my paper clip) and was able to breathe.

Just for today, I will image myself as a paper clip and stay fully upright in the center of my "tile" (my life).

October 6 ⁓ *Schmoozing*

"Can we talk?"

—Joan Rivers

Schmoozing, or chatting informally, helps create a spirit-friendly work culture. When appropriate, schmoozing is positive and allows us to share our stories. It creates a space in which people feel safe to reveal themselves.

Derrick had been raised to be a private person and not to be nosy. Because he did not schmooze with his superiors, they weren't entirely comfortable with increasing Derrick's responsibilities: they didn't feel they "knew" him. Derrick recognized the problem and decided that if he wanted to achieve his professional goals, he had to learn to schmooze. He started slowly, inquiring about employees' families and their outside interests. After attending the funeral of a co-worker's father and sending a congratulatory card when another employee had a baby, Derrick was shocked to see the responses from his fellow employees. He learned that schmoozing did not mean that he was prying or nosy as he had thought. Derrick opened the door to his spirit, and in the process, he liked himself better. And so did his employers; he soon received the promotion.

Just for today, I will take time to schmooze, to get to know someone just a little bit better, knowing we will both gain from the connection in many ways.

"There is always room for those who can be relied upon to deliver the goods when they say they will."

—Napoleon Hill

How believable, or credible, are the leaders in your workplace? We know that companies, like people, have reputations, and these reputations are based on how credible they are in their dealings with people.

When Jack went to work in a young high-tech firm, he was surprised to see how differently the workplace was from what all the company's marketing material had said. Jack's boss showed him a graph about workplace productivity. It indicated that those workers who fell at the tail end of the graph would have one year to "shape up" or be fired. Jack was shocked; he had heard this was a "learning organization." Jack became keenly aware that he had joined a fear-driven organization. Its leaders did not seem to care about the intellectual capital brought to them from the outside and actually watched that capital leave. Jack himself soon left for another job, and he was relieved to know he made a wise choice—the company he left went bankrupt.

Just for today, I will work on my own credibility. I will live up to the words I speak and the commitments I make.

October 8 ∽ *Contributions*

"The human contribution is the essential ingredient. It is only in the giving of oneself to others that we truly live."

—Sparky Anderson

There are so many ways to contribute in the workplace. Besides our usual contributions, some employees volunteer in the community; others organize the office food drives to stock local food shelves. Many schoolteachers also contribute their own school supplies.

When Meredith began her job as executive director of a neighborhood community center, she did not know what she was going to do for resources: funding was very limited in the poor neighborhood. Meredith turned to some people she had known through the years, inviting them on a bus tour through the neighborhood and to serve meals in a soup kitchen. When her friends saw the commitment the neighborhood residents had to their own renewal, they decided to get involved. Some gave money, others served in neighborhood agencies, and a few even joined the board of the agency. Meredith was deeply touched by the heartfelt contributions, and her spirit soared as the neighborhood residents moved forward in their renewal.

Just for today, I will renew how I make contributions and explore new possibilities.

"Pull the string, and it will follow you wherever you wish. Push it and it will go nowhere at all."

—Dwight D. Eisenhower

What do you believe are the three top essentials of leadership?

When Matt promoted Elissa, he was confident in her ability to lead a regional sales team. She had a good record in sales and presented herself confidently. When Matt later learned that Elissa's performance was slipping, he did not consider that his leadership might be part of the problem. In a meeting one day, Matt and some colleagues assessed themselves on three basic leadership roles—their ability to coach, to challenge, and to build confidence. Much to his surprise, Matt ranked himself low. His coaching of Elissa had consisted mostly of criticism! His team offered to help, and he immediately accepted their coaching. Matt began with constructively coaching Elissa and within months, her performance dramatically improved. Matt's spirit was enlivened in the process.

Just for today, I will ask myself how effectively I lead others. I will focus on the essentials and keep it simple.

October 10 ～ *Complaining*

"The stems of grievance put down their heavy roots / And by end of summer crack the pavement."

—Joseph Miles

Griping often seems widespread, coming from ourselves as well as our co-workers. But is it constructive? Two Harvard researchers, Robert Kegan and Lisa Laskow Lahey, decided to study how people interact at more than 650 organizations. In their studies over a fifteen-year period, they learned that it is possible to change complaints into the starting point for both individual transformation and company change. If we look at what's underneath a complaint—what values, assumptions, and feelings are driving it—we can detect what's missing in our workplaces. From there, we can take action to meet our needs.

Marcella griped loudly about not being included in division meetings. Reflecting on the feelings underlying her griping, she realized she valued inclusion. Thereafter, she committed to act and speak with those above her about the problem. When Marcella took responsibility for her griping, she not only honored her values but also contributed to the company's overall strength.

Just for today, I will ask myself what values, assumptions, and feelings lie behind my complaints. I will take responsibility for what I need.

"When the going gets tough, the tough get creative."

—Sheila Wellington

Adversity affects us all. It is how we respond to it that determines success or failure.

Jacinta and Romero, agency administrators, had felt confident about their plan for their proposed community center. Then suddenly the economy took a downturn, and the donor groups they had counted on pulled back, citing budget cuts. Jacinta and Romero were close to despair; the years of work to get to this point seemed wasted. They decided to turn to their advisory group and out of the adversity came a new plan: join with four other groups in town and present grant proposals for funding the center. Jacinta, Romero, and their new colleagues formed a strong "we" to take their story forward. Delayed just one year, the center did happen and was larger than originally planned. By looking for a way to carry their spirit of commitment forward, they created something better than they had imagined.

Just for today, I will trust that if I follow my spirit, I will succeed in adversity. There is another path if I stay committed.

October 12 ～ Cycles

"Cycles teach you patience."

—Warren G. Bennis

When we listen to the elders in business who have sustained their companies through many changes, we often hear the word *cycles*. These elders comment that they have learned patience by living through cycles.

Patience did not come easily to young Lao Ming, who had to lay off thousands of employees. He feared the public would think he was simply saving money and taking their manufacturing to Asia—which was not the case. He went to see his mentor, a business elder with a good heart, who suggested that Lao read the book *The Living Company* by Arie de Geus. The book argues that a living company can and does renew itself through the years, much like a healthy family does. Lao realized that he had to practice patience and think positively about the direction in which they were moving. By facing his fear, he was able to stay in touch with his spirit.

Just for today, I will practice patience when I am tempted to enter into fear because of change. It may perhaps be just another cycle of life.

Panic ⌒ October 13

"When you panic, your brain shuts down; you stop listening and learning."

—William F. Miller

Most of us have experienced change that creates panic. Panic comes from deep-seated fears, or what we often call "phantom fears."

Jacob, whose company manufactured automobile parts, went into a state of panic when he learned that he might be losing his largest contract. His company had had the privilege of being the automaker's number one supplier of certain parts, and he never dreamed that they could lose this account. Many people's livelihoods depended on this contract. Jacob knew his company had managed the account well; he did not see any possibility of changing their price structures; and he knew he had a good relationship with the auto manufacturer. The representative told Jacob that he would let him know—"We are making major changes here under new leadership." At first Jacob felt paralyzed. He soon realized that he had shut down totally; he could not think. He turned to sitting in silence and did some deep breathing. He then went to his partner, and together they listed four possible strategies. With concrete plans to do their best to retain the account, his panic faded.

Just for today, I will ask myself what fears in me might create panic. I will use my inner resources to calm my anxieties and know that I will survive any outcomes.

October 14 ～ *Criticism*

"Criticism is an indirect form of self-boasting."

—Dr. Emmit Fox

Criticism comes easily to many of us—at least when it comes to criticizing others. Often we are not aware of how unfair we are in our criticism. Some of us may criticize to make ourselves feel superior.

When Sara was preparing her speech for the company's annual meeting, she sent a copy of it to her boss, Kurt. Kurt immediately red-inked her speech, converting her message to his own. Sara was devastated when she received Kurt's edit of her speech; the meeting was the very next day! She had sent it as information, not for critique. Sara became anxious; she had to act. She called Kurt with her concern and then went to see him. She asserted that she was not opposed to criticism, but to sound so absolute in his criticism seemed like a personal attack. To her surprise, Kurt listened carefully and then admitted that he had been feeling competitive with her and owed her an apology. Sara felt a deep sense of relief and self-respect. They shook hands and prepared together for their presentations. Sara had honored her spirit and had given Kurt a gift.

Just for today, I will be mindful of how I criticize and how genuine the criticism is. Is it to help another or to raise myself up?

"He feels the need of it [transitions], more, he loves it; for the instability, instead of meaning disaster to him, seems to give birth only to miracles all about him."

—Alexis de Tocqueville

How often do you hear people say, "Well, we are in transition" in response to criticism. Our life transitions affect our work lives, and our work transitions affect our personal lives. The question is, when are we not in transition? In the world of nature, transitions are obvious: we see the flower blossoming or the bird molting. In our work lives, the effects of transitions are far-reaching as Dina's story shows.

Dina was well aware that she was in transition; she had left a job of twelve years and had several opportunities before her. She took her time, moving to a new city and exploring her options carefully. She rented an apartment rather than buying, and, most important, she spoke at length with her friends about her feeling of uprootedness. She grieved her losses and explored her next move. By facing the transition with care, she found buried talents surfacing. In time, she felt at peace with her new life.

Just for today, I will ask myself whether I am in transition in work or in my personal life. I'll also consider what inner resources I have to cope with the in-between.

October 16 ⌒ *Business Mortality*

"Youth is a gift of nature, but age is a work of art."

—Garson Kanin

Have you ever wondered why American businesses have a life expectancy of no more than forty to fifty years—less than the life span of a human being? When Arie de Geus researched why some companies lived for hundreds of years while others died so early, he found some definite patterns. Successful companies, he learned, focused more on tending to their employees than producing a more competitive "widget."

Manuel and Jose had been running their family business since they were in their early twenties. Now, as they were bringing the fifth generation into the business, they realized that their product—a sewing machine part—would eventually be phased out of the newer models. Worried about their loyal employees, they held a company-wide meeting and together they assessed their pooled talents. After some research, they entered a new business—manufacturing home alarm systems. The employees were enthusiastic; they willingly took pay cuts the first year. Within two years, with renewed spirits, they were financially successful. But more than that, they felt the exuberance of remaining a "living company."

Just for today, I will ask myself what attitude I bring to my work to keep it "living." I will commit to do my part to contribute in all work systems toward a "living company."

"What you don't do can be a destructive force."

—Eleanor Roosevelt

Slothfulness is one of the top five contributors to blocking spiritual growth at work. Sluggishness creates a workplace with the "flattened spirits syndrome."

Rachel did not understand why so many employees, of various ages, at her large law firm seemed to be either discouraged or lazy. They did not take the initiative; they always waited to receive direction. Rachel, a senior partner, didn't know whether they were bored or if they were just plain lazy. They seemed not to care about their work. Feeling as if she had nothing to lose, she conducted an employee satisfaction survey and follow-up group meetings. The work groups said they needed music and art—and more company parties. Rachel implemented their suggestions, and soon the changes were obvious. At the company get-togethers, the employees learned more about one another; this created a more friendly work culture and seemed to energize the employees. They now helped each other out, and laughter could be heard more readily in the workplace. The addition of music and artwork in the work environment also contributed to the new culture. With the new spirit of cooperation, the slothfulness was transformed into caring.

Just for today, I will consider how and where I experience slothfulness. I will experiment by caring about my co-workers, or at least "acting as if" I care, and notice the difference.

October 18 〜 *Red-Ink Behaviors*

"He that scattereth thorns must not go barefoot."

—Thomas Fuller

Business is haunted by the high cost of "red-ink be-haviors," a phrase coined by Jean Hollands in her book by the same name. Red-ink behaviors are problem behaviors that create cultures of disrespect—arrogance, intimidation, perfectionism, victimization, non-team at-titudes, micromanagement, and triangular "games." Such behaviors block spiritual growth in our workplaces.

When Mitchell took over a large paper company, he learned quickly about the red-ink behaviors that per-vaded the company. He was shocked to hear about the rude and shaming language plant managers used with employees. Some managers drank beer in their office meetings; womanizing was rampant. Absenteeism was high; spirits were low. Mitchell decided to hire a training company to help implement behavioral changes through-out the workplace, and he knew well enough to start at the top. Within two years, about thirty people had re-signed; those who remained were off to a new and better start.

Just for today, I will ask myself whether and how I contribute to red-ink behaviors. If I witness such behaviors, I will take action.

"A wise man will make more opportunities than he finds."

—Francis Bacon

Have you ever considered what legacy you would like to leave in your workplace? Perhaps you've found a better way of doing some routine task, initiated a lending library at work, or created a ritual.

Gladdie was preparing to leave her long-term career as a bookkeeper. Her work had meant a lot to her. She used to say, "Well, I wasn't born here, but I did grow up here." Gladdie decided she wanted to pass on to others the opportunity to learn. She had managed to save a small nest egg that she would not need in her retirement. She went to her company's owner and together they set up the Gladdie Williams's scholarship—a scholarship for young women to have a paid bookkeeping internship in the firm. The scholarship would support a partial salary for the interns while they studied for a degree in accounting. Gladdie felt a warm glow as she signed the papers for her legacy.

Just for today, I will think about what legacy I would like to leave—tangible or intangible.

October 20 ⌒ *Addiction*

"Strange! That what is enjoyed without pleasure cannot be discontinued without pain."

—Hannah More

Addictions are often lurking in companies. They may be in the form of workaholism, eating disorders, gambling, cocaine use, or alcoholism. When there is addiction at the top, codependent behaviors swirl throughout the system.

None of Stuart's colleagues thought much of the silver decanters that lined his office shelf. What they did notice were his afternoon mood swings that caused everyone to walk on eggshells. Nancy had never thought much about Stuart's temperament until she walked into his office when his door was ajar and saw him put aside his glass so quickly that he spilled liquor on the carpet. Flushed, he attempted some small talk. Nancy's awareness came like a bolt. Having grown up with alcoholism, she saw the obvious root of Stuart's behavior. Nancy cared about Stuart; she began a successful intervention process that resulted in his getting treatment. The company now faced a new challenge—to work together in a healthy system. Nancy and Stuart were leaders in the firm's spiritual renewal.

Just for today, I will focus on what addictions I notice in my work world. I promise to comment on my reality.

"Lie not, neither to thyself, nor man, nor God. It is for cowards to lie."

—George Herbert

Have you ever experienced dishonesty at work? How and when we choose to name or confront a dishonest behavior can be a challenge.

When Robbie attended a team meeting in which the next team leader would be chosen, she knew something was not right; she could feel it. When someone presented her name for team leader, she felt some tension in the air. Her intuition told her that one or maybe two team members were being dishonest with the others when they agreed to support her nomination. Robbie knew that a team leader would not succeed without backing from the entire group and so declined the role. Following the meeting, Robbie approached a colleague, one of the "withholders," and asked him to be honest about his reluctance. Robbie was shocked to learn that her colleague had misunderstood a memo she had sent and had allowed the resulting mistrust to affect his confidence in her. Robbie, having had the courage to confront her colleague and talk it through, felt the tension fall away.

Just for today, I will ask myself how and when I am dishonest in my relationships at work. I'll consider what I can do to honor my spirit.

October 22 ⟿ *Part-Time Work*

"The spirit is an inward flame; a lamp the world blows upon but never puts out."

—Margot Asquith

Have you ever been a part-time worker? Those who work in permanent, in-house jobs have a sense of belonging. But for those who work in temporary or part-time jobs, the work world is often filled with isolation.

Sahid drove a taxi while attending school for a degree in computer science. He said that driving a taxi allowed him time to do his book studies, yet, as an immigrant, he felt lonely in his new city. His goals were related to his future career—not his current job—and so his energy wasn't focused on connecting strongly with his work world. One day, Sahid found a daily meditation book that a customer had left in the back of his cab. He found that the daily meditations were very comforting to him. The little book became a good friend to Sahid; he no longer felt alone. As long as he could stay in touch with his spirituality, he could be with himself in a new and comforting way.

Just for today, I will focus on nurturing my spirit when I don't feel that I belong.

"Some people are making such thorough plans for rainy days that they aren't enjoying today's sunshine."

—William Faulkner

Just what is on your agenda today? Roberta was a thorough agenda planner. Analytical and very focused, she felt challenged when the president said the company wanted to move toward a more democratic leadership system. Roberta doubted her capacity to do this. When Roberta entered a meeting with her direct reports, clipboard and pen in hand, one of the senior men, Mike, said, "Roberta, we know that you have a full agenda that probably suits our work options well, but we want to do something different today. We want to process how we make decisions as a group."

"What do you mean, *process?*" she queried.

"We want to talk as a group about how we interact together with our agenda plans. And, remember," he smiled, "this fits with our revised vision."

Suddenly Roberta softened and said, "Okay, guys; I guess we can just put this agenda aside today and talk together. I want you to know that I am a learner in this, so I will need your help."

Just for today, I will look at how I balance my agendas, my rational planning, with the more natural process of life that brings opportunities for growth.

October 24   ∽   *Best Practices*

"It is not who is right, but what is right, that is of importance."

—Thomas H. Huxley

Sometimes people are so involved in performing well at their particular jobs that they don't even realize that what they do contributes to the company's "best practices"—the documented strategies and tactics that earn a company its reputation.

Irv decided to examine how well his family-run company was doing. His brother and business partner, Mel, thought "It isn't broken, so don't fix it." But Irv was serious about their company's reputation for excellence. He persisted and decided to look at organizations in other industries. He used data that was already available in the company's employee development, customer service, and human resources departments to compare progress. Within just three months, Irv and Mel had learned enough new practices from outside industries that their employees began to notice and appreciate the changes the brothers were making.

Just for today, I will ask myself about my own "best practices" and whether I am incorporating my highest self into my work life.

"As for the future, your task is not to foresee it, but to enable it."

—Antoine de Saint-Exupery

Do you realize that you are now living in a future you once enabled? How often do we ignore the fact that today is not only our present, but our past's future?

Once, when traveling in East Africa, I saw a native tribesman standing motionless on one leg (one wrapped around the other) with perfect balance. Hours later, when we saw him in the exact same place, I asked our guide what the man was doing. "Oh," the guide said simply, "he is waiting to see what life brings." I smiled, thinking about planning futures and rushing toward them, perhaps missing what life brings today. The art of life is finding a balance between planning for the future and standing still to see what life brings us today. By experiencing the moment, while keeping clear intentions of we want for the future, we live life to its fullest.

Just for today, I will pay attention to the richness of today—a richness I can take with me to create the future.

October 26 ～ *Change Agents*

"One doesn't discover new lands without consenting to lose sight of the shore for a very long time."

—André Gide

Have you ever considered yourself to be an agent of change? Who is the person at your work that typically comes up with the ideas, the strategies for change?

Alexis was a true change agent. She was curious, highly intelligent, and a risk taker. She was comfortable in her view that not all changes would work well. When two high-cost projects that she had initiated failed, her peer group wanted to blame her. But an outside facilitator helped them discover that while Alexis was certainly the identified change agent, the rest of the group was responsible for giving feedback and perhaps saying no to some projects. The group members had not realized that they had failed to be responsible. At the meeting's end, they apologized to Alexis for allowing her to take the risks for them without their support. They also committed to helping Alexis carry out future ideas; their sense of team took another step forward.

Just for today, I will ask myself in what areas I am a change agent. If I participate in the changes of another, I'll consider how well I share the responsibility.

"A moral choice in its basic terms appears to be a choice that favors survival: a choice made in favor of life."

—Ursula K. Le Guin

We often hear today about thinking globally and acting locally. In what ways are you challenged to think globally in your workplace? To engage in global thinking does not mean that we travel monthly to foreign lands, but that we think about the rest of the world—that we are global citizens and global workers.

Jessie's job as marketing director was to watch over global markets, looking for solid business opportunities. When he discovered a company that could manufacture parts for them in the south of India, he knew that he had to do an assessment first. The economic assessment showed the move was a good one—good for the village and good for the village economics. But when he did the moral assessment, his findings were not as glowing. He knew he would be supporting child labor and that shifting parts production to India would take jobs from his own country. So his company did not sign the deal. Jessie's work group told him how proud they were of him for including morality and ethics in his global thinking.

Just for today, I will remind myself that I belong to the world, and to a world of nations. As a responsible world citizen, I must treat my global friends with respect in thought and action.

October 28 ⌒ *Pathways*

"Some men go through a forest and see no firewood."

—English proverb

Have you ever had to create a fresh pathway? One group admitted they felt stuck. Their group leader, Tim, asked them to close their eyes and allow images about where they were to enter their minds. One said she saw a dark forest with trees so close together there was no pathway; another person reported seeing a huge pile of sludge. The rest of the images were just as discouraging. Tim then asked them to close their eyes again. With music playing softly in the background, he led them through an exercise of guided imagery. He asked the employees to picture themselves with a dark forest behind them as they stood in a sunny clearing and looked out at a range of mountains with many pathways. He instructed them to unpack their bags. They were to leave behind what they no longer needed and repack the items that served them well. The last part of the exercise included naming who was there with them to provide support. A concluding group discussion revealed that the entire group came up with a fresh pathway, a sense of direction, support, and a united spirit.

Just for today, I will ask myself what new pathways might be in front of me. By looking forward, and not back, I can stay focused on my spiritual direction.

"Promise a lot and give even more."

—Anthony J. D'Angelo

When have you had to break a promise? Louise faced a painful task; she was to meet with one of her top employees, Victoria, and explain why she would not receive the promotion that Louise and her partners had promised to her. Louise had been meeting regularly with Victoria's group to develop a team, yet she knew that she could not effectively lead the group after letting down Victoria. Louise, a contained, brisk businesswoman, met with the entire group, including Victoria, to discuss the situation openly. Louise began with a slow pace, carefully choosing her words as she told the story. Sitting directly in front of Victoria, she suddenly began crying. "There is no way, Victoria, that you deserve to be treated like this; let me explain how dreadfully mistaken we were." As Louise continued to tell her story with painful truth, Victoria and the other group members were touched to tears with her sincerity. The group had never dreamed that Louise could be that real; her remorse was visible. They thanked Louise for her authentic leadership.

Just for today, I will focus on keeping my promises to people. If I fail to keep my word, I will reach closure by being brave enough to explain what truly happened.

October 30 ~ *Intellectual Capital*

"If you really do put a small value upon yourself, rest assured that the world will not raise your price."

—Anonymous

Have you ever assessed what your intellectual capital is? Or what it is worth? Many organizations today are assessing what intellectual capital costs, especially during large layoffs, mergers, and acquisitions. How many years of talent and knowledge leave an organization when employees are released so easily?

Narunja had operated her own small business for years and then began to work as a consultant to various businesses. Through the years, she had developed highly usable, successful models for helping people measure their own growth. When she finished a highly successful presentation to a firm wanting to learn from her, they asked her to come work with them. When Narunja spoke with friends about the offer, she realized that in her generous spirit, she had neglected to place a value on the intellectual capital that she had grown through the years. She met with the company again, this time with a price for the capital she brought. When their agreement was solidified, they moved forward in a win-win partnership.

Just for today, I will recognize the strength of my intellectual capital and know when I am to give it freely and when I should charge for it. I will honor my spiritual wealth.

Masking ∽ October 31

"It's always the rug you've been sweeping things under that gets pulled out from under you."

—Bannerman

Do you know when you are putting on a mask? Halloween is fun for many because we can deliberately wear a mask and hide our true selves. On other occasions, most of us have put on a mask—perhaps because we did not feel safe, were experiencing personal pain, or felt the timing was just not right.

Harriet had never realized how masked she was. Tall, slender, with a dignified presence, she reeked of competence. Then Harriet participated in a seminar with an outside trainer in which they reviewed their childhood experiences. Suddenly, Harriet became in touch with the person behind the mask, the person she had been hiding. That person felt insecure and fearful that others would learn she was an "incompetent fraud." The trainer saw her vulnerability and offered to work with her privately. Soon, Harriet was relieved to see how her mask had also helped her survive a painful childhood. Within a few months, Harriet learned how to remove the mask that had blocked her true spirit—the spirit she now befriended.

Just for today, I will ask myself how I mask myself and with whom, so I can learn more about what might be blocking my spirit.

November

"Yes, I do touch. I believe that everyone needs that."

—Diana, princess of Wales

How high, or common, is the touch in your workplace? There are many ways in which to touch one another. We see people touching one another through sincere handshakes and respectful embraces. At the same time, we know that physical touch is not welcomed by all and can even be disrespectful. Many people have learned the hard way that one person's desire to nurture is another person's moment of terror.

When Marisa accepted a new job, she immediately noticed how "high touch" the company was. Having worked through experiences of early childhood sexual abuse, she was still fearful of physical touch and so kept her guard up somewhat. To her surprise, she soon was pleased with the informality of the organization and the warmth she felt from the group who brought her on board. She learned how creatively they handled the high-touch concept. She received e-mails of welcome during her first week. She saw people touch others through direct eye contact and warm words of appreciation for small tasks. Marisa felt safe and knew that her spirit could grow there.

Just for today, I will be respectful of what high touch means for others as well as for myself and find creative expressions of touch.

November 2 ⁀ *Good-heartedness*

"The first condition of human goodness is something to love; the second, something to reverence."

—George Eliot

How do you experience good-heartedness at work? When Al learned that Eddie, one of his key employees, was diagnosed with cancer and had to undergo chemotherapy immediately, he acted quickly. He made certain that the medical costs would be covered, and he formed a small support circle within the company who would take turns visiting Eddie. As the treatment failed and the end of life approached, Eddie returned to work for a few days to share his life lessons with his co-workers, focusing on how his cancer had changed his life. Others then came forth with their own untold painful experiences and life threats. Eddie's colleagues received a precious gift from Eddie's final advice and words of inspiration. Although the experience was painful, it was nonetheless enriching. Most important, Eddie's last days were filled with peace and comfort in knowing that his family would be taken care of, greatly due to the company's good-heartedness.

Just for today, I will ask myself how I practice good-heartedness in my work. I will write down good-hearted acts that I witness.

Ideas ∽ November 3

"It is a dangerous thing to have an idea that you will not practice."

—Phyllis Bottome

Do you live in a world of ideas? Do new ideas excite you? Do you work in an environment where ideas are welcomed and not judged prematurely?

Helene was a bit surprised when a group of information technology (IT) specialists in her scientific research firm wanted to meet with her. She had often teasingly commented on how difficult it was to lead people who were younger and smarter than she was. When they presented their idea—to reorganize their department reporting structures—she felt her ego swaying. She wondered whether she was losing control and contemplated whether her employees would still respect her if she acknowledged that they had a better idea than their leader could come up with. Helene knew the proposed system would change her role greatly. She was also aware of the high turnover in IT positions and how in demand these good employees were. Helene breathed deeply, replying, "Well that sounds like a fine idea. Let's work together on making it happen." Helene's acceptance of this new idea marked another step in her spiritual growth.

Just for today, I will be respectful of new ideas, both my own and others, and take the risk to discuss them with others.

November 4 ~ *Alternative Thinking*

"In creating, the only hard thing's to begin; a grass-blade's no easier to make than an oak."

—James Russell Lowell

Are you ever willing to risk thinking in new ways? When Nancy and Nydia attended a conference on global awareness and workplace diversity, they returned excited to consider alternatives for conducting their Internet business. At the conference, they had learned about the Grameen Bank, a bank that some years ago started giving credit to people in the developing world. Nancy and Nydia realized that their company could benefit from hiring people in India to monitor technology systems; it did not matter whether their employees lived in India or in Idaho. The women contacted the Grameen Bank in Bangladesh and explored opportunities in some small villages. The Grameen Bank lauded them for working to bring people out of poverty through an entrepreneurial connection. Nancy and Nydia faced another challenge, however—convincing their own company that hiring and developing people in India would be a good move. With committed spirits, Nancy and Nydia did their homework, made a solid presentation, and won the management team's approval.

Just for today, I will consider how I can think alternatively. I will tune into new ways of thinking.

"Energy is equal to desire and purpose."

—Sheryl Adams

Does your work give you energy, or does it drain you of energy? If we look closely at our energy levels, we'll learn much about our spiritual growth. Have you ever witnessed a highly energetic child playing outside, or someone who can hike for hours without an energy drain? We can read energy in our bodies quite readily. You can feel energy in a handshake, in a walk. Our energy levels at work are often closely related to our purpose. When we are clear about our purpose, and can stay focused on that purpose, we will experience high energy.

Until Matt took the time to reflect on what his purpose was in his telecommunications work, his energy level was low; work was just plain *work* to him. There was little joy. After participating in a seminar on purpose, he decided to write his out. It was quite simple: "To help people grow." As Matt focused daily on his higher purpose, his energy level soared. Matt was grateful that he had found his purpose and a closer connection to his spirit.

Just for today, I will focus on what ignites my energy, what brings me satisfaction and joy, and take note of what I have little energy for.

November 6 ⁓ *Boldness*

"Whatever you can do, or dream you can, begin it. Boldness has genius, power, and magic in it."

—Johann Wolfgang von Goethe

How does boldness enter your workplace? Whatever our work is, there are opportunities for boldness. Reverend Cecil Williams of San Francisco's Glide Memorial Church knows about making bold decisions. Back in 1963, his church was on the edge of extinction; the attendance at Sunday services was down to thirty-five people. He decided to increase membership and not be fussy. His new members included prostitutes and drug addicts, fitting his purpose to transform Glide into a catalyst for community action and social change. The new membership today includes gays, lesbians, dotcommers, the homeless, and a mix of all colors—and all ages. The national leadership at first held Glide at arm's length, but today they boast about this model of community. Cecil Williams's bold work with Glide Memorial Church has truly ignited spirits; his congregation now includes ten thousand people, and its members are involved in more than fifty community service programs.

Just for today, I will consider where and how I can be bold and take the risks necessary to make one small difference in the world.

"If you want to capture people's attention—during a presentation or while chatting on a plane—you have to give a great performance."

—Curtis Sittenfeld

How do you feel when you are asked to make a presentation at work? Most people report experiencing a great deal of anxiety over making presentations. Presentation coaches know that audiences remember less than 10 percent of what they see, do, and hear. This means that when we are presenting, we must be captivating. That does not happen through words alone; it happens through the energy we convey.

Phyllis's new job required her to frequently give presentations, an area she considered herself weak in. She knew she had to learn how to master some defeating inner messages. Phyllis turned to theater techniques to improve her performance skills. She recognized that her thoughts dominated her presence and knew she had to make changes. She learned to convert her inner dialogue into positive messages while she spoke, saying to herself, "I love my work," followed by, "I am comfortable in doing this." When put into practice, her new internal dialogue process was extremely helpful; her whole self was at work and her presentations became powerful.

Just for today, I will pay attention to my performance when I'm presenting myself in small conversations or in public speaking. I will focus on being real and make room for my spiritual expression.

November 8 ～ *Professional Development*

"What is the most rigorous law of our being? Growth. No smallest atom of our moral, mental, or physical structure can stand still a year. It grows; it must grow. Nothing can prevent it."

—Mark Twain

Does your work environment support professional development? For many, professional development seems like a luxury item, yet studies show that when chosen carefully, professional development can truly enhance one's performance and productivity.

Duncan had been reluctant to budget for professional development for his employees. When two workers, Cynthia and Bud, asked to attend a seminar, he hedged. "How will we know the worth of that week?" he asked. Cynthia and Bud almost simultaneously exclaimed, "Well, what if we bring you back an oral presentation of our discoveries?" After the seminar, they enthusiastically presented the material that they saw as cutting edge. The other group members responded to their excitement and worked to integrate some of the thinking into their workplace.

The next year, Duncan budgeted in twice as much money for professional development. He appreciated how the spirit of two employees ignited the spirits of two hundred.

Just for today, I will pay attention to my professional development and seek what I need. As I learn new ideas, my spirit soars.

"Until women assume the place in society which good sense and good feeling alike assign to them, human improvement must advance but feebly."

—Francis Wright

When we read that women lead only two Fortune 500 companies, what questions does that raise? Futurist Nancy Ramsey predicts that at the current rate of social change, women won't achieve full equality in the workplace with men until the year 2270. Because they recognize limitations in corporations, more American women currently work for women-owned businesses than for the Fortune 500.

Bob's firm believed that they treated their employees fairly and had fair hiring practices. Yet they hired only white people and men held all of the key positions. They told themselves that women would not want to work in their culture because of its "high-tech" focus. In a side conversation one day, a consultant confronted Bob and suggested that he attend a seminar on diversity. Bob "got it" and soon became an advocate for women at work, recognizing that his influence could be felt within the company and also within the industry. With dramatic hiring changes, Bob and his employees transformed their culture to be diverse through inclusion.

Just for today, I will be aware of women at work and support new ways for women to create their own opportunities.

November 10 ～ *Organizational Change*

"Organizations don't change; people do."

Have you ever noticed how often people talk about organizational change as though a machine were being repaired or reengineered? Organizational change takes time; it requires commitment; and it involves people.

When Ken agreed to attend a fund-raising business luncheon for Tibetans and to hear the Dalai Lama (a spiritual leader in exile from Tibet) speak, he did not have any expectations. Yet Ken was surprised at how the messages affected him. The Dalai Lama opened his talk by addressing those who had been with him before. He asked, "What has changed since we last met?" Ken, who had heard him speak four years earlier, reflected on his own company and silently said, "Not much." When the Dalai Lama then spoke of "internal disarmament," Ken thought of all the war metaphors in his company. And when he talked about how our attachments keep us stuck in old ways, Ken experienced an exciting "aha." Ken realized why he was really there and he immediately began thinking about how his company's upcoming organizational change could encompass spiritual principles. These principles eventually led to a new work culture.

Just for today, I will ask myself how I apply my spiritual growth to organizational change.

"Make your life a mission, not an intermission."

—Arnold H. Glasgow

How many times have you heard your co-workers talk about the old, worn mission statement that hangs on the wall in the front office?

Penny had agreed to lead the creation of a mission statement for her division of a large retail store. She knew that the place to start was with their reason for being and that they should address three questions: Who are we? Why do we exist? What do we do? She had a good working model, starting with the company's values. Then it occurred to Penny that the corporate mission was simply not enough. Penny asked the group to do something different, to take a risk. She asked the group members to write their own personal mission statements—responding to the three questions: Who am I? Why do I exist? What do I do here? This personal mission assignment greatly affected the working dynamics of the group. By identifying their own personal mission, the employees could embark on their corporate mission wholeheartedly, with spirit.

Just for today, I will take time to write my own personal mission and know that wherever I work, my mission is my constant companion.

November 12 ⌒ *Passion*

"Passions are vices or virtues to their highest powers."

—Johann Wolfgang von Goethe

In what ways and at what times have you known passion in your work or in your hobbies? In an ideal world, our passion would be our paid work, but that's not always the case.

Cliff sought professional coaching because of his passion—his antique boat hobby. His angry wife had nudged him to seek help because his passion consumed the majority of his free time and took extra family funds. His remaining time went into his paid work as a freelance consultant. The toll for Cliff's passion had mounted: his wife had threatened to leave him, and his children were acting out. He felt guilty, and yet his passion drove him. Cliff cared deeply about his wife and family and became actively involved in the coaching process. Cliff felt understood and knew he had to learn to balance his paid work with his passion. He committed to behavioral changes, managed his time successfully, and talked with his coach weekly. This was difficult for Cliff, but with his family's support, he soon achieved balance. Cliff realized that without his guilt, he could enjoy his passion even more and be open to growth—financially and spiritually.

Just for today, I will ask myself where my passions lie and how I work with my passions to create a full life.

"The need for change bulldozed a road down the center of my mind."

—Maya Angelou

How many people have you seen turn to another career in their fifties? Because we live longer and work more years than previous generations, many of us find ourselves getting bored with our careers and become unable to imagine doing them for another twenty years.

When Adam turned down a big promotion that meant a move to New York, he thought he would be satisfied with his "settled-in life." But within months after saying no, he felt flat. His financial service business no longer stimulated him. He decided to cut back hours at his business and began working for a non-profit agency in the community. Once again, Adam felt alive—he was learning and growing. He had never dreamt he would be developing a "parallel career," as Peter Drucker calls it, at this stage in his life. He had thought those new careers were for the young folks, but by seeking a change, Adam found stimulation and an enlivened spirit.

Just for today, I will ask myself what keeps my spirit alive at work and what opportunities might be available for service and growth.

November 14 ～ *Servant Leadership*

"The best way to find yourself is to lose yourself in the service of others."

—Mahatma Gandhi

Have you ever thought about what the popular term *servant leadership* means? Some years ago Robert Greenleaf, a retired AT&T executive, wrote a book entitled *Servant Leadership*. The premise of the book was that whether you are a shop supervisor or a world leader, your responsibility is to serve your constituents. With this in place, leadership comes naturally.

Barry had learned his dad's military leadership style well; he was hierarchical and controlling. But when Barry's wife died of cancer, his world fell apart and his life changed dramatically. His loss hit him deeply. As a single parent of two young boys, he was overwhelmed. He took time out and learned a lot about himself, including his leadership style. As he shifted to servant leadership—committed to the growth of his employees and to making them shine—he soon had dedicated followers who were creative, healthy, and resourceful. Barry could hardly recognize himself as he reflected on the man he used to be. Letting go opened Barry's heart to his boys, his employees, and his spirit.

Just for today, I will assess what I bring to servant leadership— how I help develop those with whom I work. My spirit and the spirits of those around me can shine with servant leadership.

"The best thing we do in life is when we do good to others and get nothing in return—for the good will be waiting for us in the end."

—Mama D.

At times, our need to support loved ones in their career decisions should outweigh our concerns about day-to-day life; we need to look at the bigger picture and appreciate where each of us is on our journey.

Mary had landed her dream job as a flight attendant on a charter airline that required her to travel internationally for weeks at a time. Although she had major responsibilities at home—three children under the age of seven, three dogs, and a husband who worked full-time—and was leaving a higher paying job in a law firm, she knew that if she didn't take the job, she wouldn't be following her heart. Though extremely leery of becoming a single parent for extended periods, Mary's husband, Bill, agreed to the transition. He realized it would be difficult but also knew that if he did not support Mary and her dreams, their relationship might suffer in other ways. After six weeks of training and two months of travel, Mary decided that spending so much time away from her family was less than desirable. She quit her job on her own terms—not Bill's—and therefore left feeling good about her decision. Mary trusted her feelings about her choices; Bill trusted the process.

Just for today, I will know that I cannot hold others back without causing damage. I will trust that when I give my support freely, the outcome will be in everyone's highest good.

November 16 ~ *Sexual Orientation*

"These names: gay, queer, homosexual are limiting. I would love to finish with them."

—Derek Jarman

Some companies encourage and support the hiring and promotion of people who are gay and lesbian, while others seem to encourage a "closet" approach.

When Sue was up for tenure at her university, she and many of her colleagues wondered whether she would pass through since she was open about her lesbianism. Sue's teaching record was remarkable, and students waited to get into her classes, but Sue knew there were closeted gays at the university. She was also aware of the beliefs held by many of the priest educators at the Catholic university. She feared that her sexual orientation might influence the administrators' decision. Sue was skeptical about her chances; she was prepared to leave and go elsewhere; she knew that her spirit could not survive in a workplace that did not honor her lifestyle. But Sue did receive tenure, and she was subsequently honored at a faculty tea. Some of her colleagues wanted to alert the local media to Sue's success as a lesbian educator, but Sue said no. The university had respected her academic excellence and rewarded her appropriately; her sexual orientation was irrelevant.

Just for today, I will be conscious that we are all human beings and that people should not be judged because of their sexual orientation.

"The more man meditates upon good thoughts, the better will be his world and the world at large."

—Confucius

Some people tease about having "bad hair days"; others of us worry more about having "bad talk days." Our self-talk determines the kind of day we will have. Most of us have at least two "voices" that speak to us, and they are often at opposite ends of the spectrum. For instance, in my writing work, I talk to myself constantly. My self-talk ranges from disparaging messages such as "I bet my agent will not like this book proposal; I can't really write" to very positive affirmations: "You really are doing a fine job; this is good stuff." My choice of self-talk affects not only my mood, but also my spiritual growth. If we want to be our own good friend, we can take charge of our day by giving ourselves affirmative messages.

Just for today, I will give myself affirmative self-talk messages. I will stay true to my spiritual growth.

November 18 ~ *Intention*

"All behavior is intentional."

—Anonymous

We are not always aware of our intentions when interacting with co-workers. Yet our behaviors certainly affect the health of our work relationships and our work environment.

Nancy was a spontaneous person and was often quick to express opinions and make comments to her co-workers. At times her casual, humorous style rankled those around her. At a communication seminar, Nancy learned about intentions and how they can drive behavior at an unconscious level. Back at the office, she decided to use a journal to focus on her unconscious intentions. First, Nancy wrote what she did or said during her daily interactions. For example, "When I learned of Jackie's promotion, I said that I bet Jackie was glad that Norma had turned it down." Nancy then wrote that her outward intention was to affirm Jackie, but her unconscious intention was to remind her that she was the second choice—thus using power over her. In time, Nancy came to recognize how many of her statements and actions had hidden intentions. Armed with that knowledge, she began to work on making her behaviors congruent with her conscious intentions. Her spirit warmed.

Just for today, I will consider the intentions behind my behaviors. I will hold myself accountable to be congruent.

"The divorce of our so-called spiritual life from our daily activities is a fatal dualism."

—M. P. Follett

Spirit refers to that vital principle or animating force within living beings, often contrasted with nonliving matter. We usually refer to the spirit as the intangible core of a person, or the soul. Often we see spirit in the eyes of another; poets describe the eyes as the windows to the spirit or soul.

When Bascal started his new job, his co-workers immediately noticed his whistling. At first people thought him a bit strange, to be that openly happy in the office. But he was happy for a reason, and Bascal had no intention of keeping it to himself. In time, Bascal invited people in his division to join him over lunch in talking about spiritual matters. He began the first meetings with readings, and people responded by discussing spiritual issues. The lunch group grew in size, and soon there were spiritual pods throughout the company. Bascal called the groups "In the Spirit of Work," and eventually, some two-thirds of the employees attended the spirit-filled meetings. In time, Bascal's whistling was drowned out by the whistling of his co-workers.

Just for today, I will allow my spirit to move freely. I will cherish my aliveness.

November 20 ⁓ *Coaching*

"The boss drives people; the leader coaches them."

—H. Gordon Selfridge

Job coaching, or active mentoring, can make a critical difference in one's career growth. Some seek coaching for a particular competency, while others turn to a coach for general skill development.

When Denise was promoted to project manager, it seemed like an obvious move: her computer skills were strong, and she was liked by her co-workers. However, her director soon received feedback from her team members that Denise didn't listen to them. The feedback suggested that Denise did not work as a team player and was lacking a key leadership skill. Denise's director asked her to get coaching for the problem, and Denise agreed. Early in the coaching contract, Denise "got it" and began to slow down, listen, and draw others out. She soon realized that not everyone thought as quickly as she did. In addition, Denise began to give positive feedback and set development goals with her employees. Within two months, there was a fresh energy in their meetings. The spirits were lively, work productivity increased, and Denise was proud of her work group.

Just for today, I will consider areas in which I may need coaching and ask for feedback from a trusted colleague. I will also recognize what coaching skills I can bring to my work with others.

Betrayal ∽ November 21

"Learning to trust is one of life's most difficult tasks."

—Isaac Watts

Betrayal in the workplace can block spiritual growth and damage our work environments in innumerable ways.

The senior management team of a mid-sized company in the Midwest had worked well together for more than twelve years. Then their business began to falter, and no one understood why. They hired a consultant, Ben, to help them evaluate their business plan and workplace dynamics. Ben immediately learned that the members of the management team gossiped about one another. He confronted them about this behavior and pointed out that when they gossiped, they were betraying each other—and the company as well. Ben helped the managers see the widespread ramifications of talking behind each other's back. The group committed to work on their honesty. Over time, they were able to speak openly to each other and business issues were addressed much more quickly. Trusting one another, they were able to move the company forward and return to profitability.

Just for today, I will focus on my behavior at work, knowing that my actions affect my co-workers and my work system. I will take responsibility for working honestly.

November 22 〜 *Illusions and Delusions*

> *"The most fatal illusion is the settled point of view. Since life is growth and motion, a fixed point of view kills anybody who has one."*
>
> —Brooks Atkinson

Illusion and delusion are closely related. The board members of one East Coast firm, a leader in its field, carried the illusion that they ran a clean, efficient, ethical company. But they deluded themselves about the behavior of their president, who had a secret life. To support his grand lifestyle and a long-term, long-distance affair, he had skimmed corporate funds. Several board members knew about the woman but not about the theft. A newer board member spoke up one day when the president was not there and confronted their delusions. "Let's face it," he said. "We are not walking our talk, and we are part of this fraud if we do not do something immediately." The board began a long and painful process to right the system, eventually uncovering the president's embezzlement and firing him. By facing their delusions, they transformed the system from spiritual bankruptcy into a culture of high principles.

Just for today, I will explore any illusions or delusions I may have about my work. What is it I do not want to let myself see?

"Nothing makes us feel so strong as a call for help."

—George Macdonald

How do you ask for help? Taylor didn't realize that she did not know how to ask for help. She had grown up in a family that saw asking for help as a sign of weakness. Taylor used to laugh at her parents' refusal to ask for help, yet unknowingly she adopted the same beliefs. Taylor was organizing her company's annual meeting for three hundred people. In the days leading up to the event, Taylor was putting in long hours and was exhausted, working every evening until 11 P.M. and returning at 5:30 A.M. Her associate Sharon was very concerned about Taylor's health. She went to Taylor's office and picked up two stacks of program materials that needed to be handled. Taylor looked up and asked, "What are you doing?" "I am going to help you with this. It is clear you cannot ask for help and that you cheat yourself from the spirit of caring," replied Sharon. Taylor immediately let go and relaxed. With a timid smile, she said, "I guess I just learned a major lesson—thanks, Sharon."

Just for today, I will recognize when I need to ask for help. I will remember that asking for help is a sign of the strength of my connection with others and not a sign of weakness.

November 24 ～ *Calling*

"Calling is the inner urge to give our gifts away."

—Dick Leider

When our life's work is an answer to our calling, our work fosters our spiritual growth.

Diane, the executive director of two philanthropy foundations, is an example of someone whose work is personally enriching. Diane's personal values of service, compassion, and national and global citizenship give her a strong foundation for her work. Although her daily work life has its ups and downs like anyone else's, she finds it quite easy to keep her spirit ignited at work. She attributes her spiritual satisfaction to three factors: First, through her interactions with other people, she meets others who are making a difference in the world. Second, the challenge of being pushed to use both her intellect and her heart provides another gift to her spirit. Finally, she feels that some of her philanthropic work inspires humanity to evolve toward a more compassionate spirit. Diane has found her calling.

Just for today, I will seek out or remind myself of my calling. I will also consider how I can further take my values and gifts to the world.

"The great thing in this world is not so much where we are but in what direction we are moving."

—Oliver Wendell Holmes Jr.

O ur work identity, who we are at work, is forged out of our work relationships over the years.

Maggie had a keen sense of who she was in every aspect of her life; she had lived in the same town and worked at the same place for many years. But when she accepted a promotion in a new city, she had a great surprise awaiting her—no one recognized her. She was an outsider. An emptiness sunk into her; she began to question the move even though it was a wonderful career opportunity. Remembering the value of all her good relationships with colleagues, she decided to take action. She e-mailed friends and asked them to stay in close touch. She journaled. She placed familiar items in her new office—photographs, awards, prints of her favorite paintings—to remind her of her identity. Maggie knew that by using temporary "supports," she could sustain her spirit during her transition period.

Just for today, I will acknowledge my work identity and give appreciation for all that has shaped me.

November 26 ~ Compensation

"Any experience can be transformed into something of value."

—Vash Young

While the dollars we earn support our basic living needs and contribute to our sense of worth, we also know that there are other forms of compensation. For some, it is a truly satisfied customer; others feel enriched by the sense of community that a workplace can provide.

Roman had never thought much about his monetary compensation; he thought he received a fair wage in his rather low-paying field. He felt respected by his organization. But Roman's "real pay," as he called it, often came from working with low-income agencies in his community. His recent objective had been to get two inner-city youth gangs talking rather than fighting—an unrealistic assignment in the eyes of many. After two years of working with the area's churches, schools, and families, Roman organized a neighborhood meeting. About thirty people were expected to attend, but three hundred came out, including many gang members. Roman's eyes filled with tears as he watched the people in this neighborhood interacting and the gang members talking. His spirit was full; he had been richly compensated for his work.

Just for today, I will examine my compensation. I will consider my spiritual compensation as well as the dollars I receive.

"When a man, a woman, see their little daily tasks as integral portions of the one great work, they are no longer drudges but co-workers with God."

—Annie Besant

What comes to mind when you think of the word *work?* For many, work is equated with drudgery, an antonym to play. But for others, work gives their lives meaning. Many people remark that they find deep satisfaction in using their innate talents to face daily challenges. Over their work lives, some will come to realize that they must change careers to fully utilize their gifts.

When Lou was in college, he had a part-time job in a foreign money exchange. After graduation, he went on to a career in international business. Along the way, however, he developed a drug problem and eventually checked himself into a drug treatment program. Following his successful treatment, he became a family therapist, working with adolescents. As Lou reviewed his work history, he noticed how his work as a therapist incorporates his talents and skills and brings him personal satisfaction. He also sees that following his gifts enables him to follow his spirit.

Just for today, I will trace my work history and examine what talents and gifts have influenced where I am today.

November 28 ～ *Submission*

"Happiness can exist only in acceptance."

—Denis de Rougemont

At times, we all have to submit to the decisions of others—perhaps an individual, perhaps a group.

Paul had worked in a university setting for many years and had learned that it was sometimes best to explore submission rather than engage in battle. He served as an adviser to Pam, a returning student who also worked on campus. When Pam became frustrated with the academic policies, she said, "I am too old to be in college." Paul replied, "Yes, you are. But the university has what you want, so you had better learn to occasionally submit and accept the system." He also told Pam that if at times she had to do something for her degree that she thought was irrelevant, she should bend her head toward the ground and wink. In that way, she would know that she was not violating her own principles but was simply working toward a degree.

Just for today, help me to realize that sometimes submission will be required of me. Submitting peacefully will help me in my spiritual growth.

"I lie to myself all the time. But I never believe me."

—S. E. Hinton

When we give voice to our beliefs and allow ourselves the privilege of thinking out loud, we hear ourselves and clarify our thinking. One way we hear ourselves is by listening closely to statements that come to our minds, whether spoken or unspoken. We also receive an opportunity to hear ourselves when we are asked to give talks and presentations at work. In both cases, our hearing often reveals our deepest thoughts. Hearing ourselves means that we are truly in touch with our inner voices.

Eddie was a telephone lineman who never took himself seriously. When Eddie learned what it meant to truly hear his own voice, he was often surprised with the statements he made. At first others would ask him, "Did you hear what you just said?" "Why, no," Eddie would reply. In time Eddie learned that hearing what he said aloud (and to himself) were gifts from his spirit and he began to take himself seriously.

Just for today, I will appreciate the times when I hear myself. I will honor my inner voice that can help guide me on my life's path.

November 30 ⌒ *Perseverance*

"Any road is bound to arrive somewhere if you follow it far enough."

—Patricia Wentworth

Where has your perseverance brought you in your life?

When Sheri was mentoring others and they asked her what had motivated her to persevere in her early years, she said, "Terror!" This response often surprised her co-workers who saw her as a confident, capable, successful manager. Yet many had not known about the hardship in Sheri's life: she had left an alcoholic husband and was in poverty for several years while she raised three young children, returned to school, and worked part time. After graduating, she worked two jobs for some time, doing whatever work was available. She indeed was not seeking purpose at this time in her life, just survival. Gradually, as she found her place in business and began earning a comfortable income without working extra jobs, she was able to relax more. As her children grew older, their demands lessened. With time at last to reflect, Sheri now recognizes the rich payoffs professionally and spiritually that she gained through her perseverance.

Just for today, I will honor perseverance. I will acknowledge that perseverance will bring spiritual rewards.

December

"It is only in the heart that anything really happens."

—Ellen Glasgow

How present is heartfulness in your work life? When Ron was preparing to return to the United States after four years of supervising a group on an oil rig, he had mixed feelings. He felt good about what his group had accomplished for the business, but he knew it would be hard to leave his co-workers and friends. When the day arrived for his farewell party, Ron felt happy and entered the hotel meeting room with deep satisfaction. He was not prepared, however, for what happened next. Seated at the front of the room—he stared when he saw the two figures—were the president and executive vice president of his company! They both wanted Ron to know how much his contributions had mattered to everyone back at the home office, and they wanted to be there to help him in his transition. Ron was deeply touched by this heartful act and promised himself that he would try to spread that spirit in his work.

Just for today, I will consider how I can express a heartful attitude to my colleagues.

December 2 ～ *Despair*

"To be truly radical is to make hope possible rather than despair convincing."

—Raymond Williams

Have you ever felt despair about your work? When Alex saw that all the energy and money he had invested in his new Internet company was sliding away before his eyes, he felt despair. When he first got into the business, "dot.com" companies were thriving, as was the stock market. He had several venture capitalists lined up to fund his life's dream and had hired some highly experienced people to help him with his new endeavor. Then the market took a downturn, and Alex was shocked at the speed with which the Internet companies began closing. He was forty-nine, not twenty-nine, and felt foolish for having invested himself so fully in this type of business. In resignation, he called his employees together and told them what they already saw coming. Together, they recognized that the universe had given them a message. After brainstorming about other business possibilities, they took the project in a new direction, and today they have a solid start-up company. Alex found that with a little help, despair can be transformed into new beginnings.

Just for today, I will recognize that transformation often lies beyond despair. All I need to bring forth is an open mind and an open spirit.

"Action, to be effective, must be directed to clearly conceived ends."

—Jawaharlal Nehru

How effective are you at work? How do your contributions make a difference?

Roger realized that he wasn't as effective as he would like to be in his executive role. He wanted to focus his talents on developing strong, ethical corporate leadership at a national level and decided that working within a large company was too plodding a method. He needed a change. First, he opened his own consulting firm, but that was also too slow. Professional effectiveness was critically important to Roger, and he knew that he had to follow his spirit. After reflecting on this for some time, he decided to make yet another move—to work for a prestigious national search firm where he could help place presidents and chief executive officers in large companies. It took Roger about two full years to begin to fully realize his effectiveness.

Just for today, I will consider how effective I am in my work. I will ask myself whether I am realizing my full potential.

December 4 ～ *Mystery*

"I step into the day. I step into my life; I step into the mystery."

—An Ojibway prayer

Where do you find mystery in your work? How often do we confuse the word *mystery* with *coincidences?*

Phyllis was very comfortable in asking "the universe" for help whenever needed. After teaching geography and yoga in Barbados for several years, she was ready for a change. Phyllis focused intently on what might be possible; she trusted life. Soon afterward, a colleague left for the States and gave her name to a fitness ranch. Phyllis was called for an interview, got the job, and has been working there for eighteen years. At the time she was leaving Barbados, many people would have called the circumstances of her upcoming move a coincidence, while Phyllis knew that her spirit was being fulfilled through the mystery in life. Little wonder that for many years Phyllis has led a program at the ranch called "The Inner Journey."

Just for today, I will be open to life and trust that the mystery can be called a coincidence in time by many. I choose to believe in the mystery.

Nurturance ⌒ December 5

"Those who we support hold us up in life."

—Marie von Ebner-Eschenbach

Do you think the word *nurturance* has a place in your work world?

Evan was up for a promotion and his company asked him to get some coaching help. While he was a "whiz" at producing bottom-line financial results, he had poor people skills. When Pat, the management coach, began working with Evan, he learned that Evan was unaware of how his past had influenced his behavior. As Pat empathetically probed Evan's childhood stories, painful memories of years of emotional abuse surfaced. Evan slowly recalled his boyhood and the feelings he had left behind. Through this work, Evan began to understand the source of his behaviors and slowly became more sensitive to others. Later, when Pat was asked to present a case study at a coaching seminar, he discussed his work with Evan. The senior leader who reviewed Pat's presentation told him, "Well, it is clear what you did—you nurtured him!" Pat smiled as he acknowledged that nurturing was a part of his work that kept his spirit alive.

Just for today, I will explore how I nurture others to sustain their spiritual growth—as well as my own.

December 6 ~ *Emotional Honesty*

"Follow the grain in your own wood."

—Howard Thurman

How emotionally honest can you be in your work life?

Ned learned quite late in life what his emotional dishonesty had cost him when a routine medical checkup revealed many symptoms of high stress, including high blood pressure. Ned's physician also reminded Ned that he had a family history of heart disease. It was time to take action or further risk his health. Ned knew the source of his stress: he had felt miserable about his work as a lawyer for the last twelve years. Yet he felt he wore "golden handcuffs" because the company benefits were exceptional. But now his children had left home, his wife was gainfully employed, and he knew at some level that it was his dishonesty—not finances—that was the real problem. Ned began taking night courses in aeronautical engineering. Within two months, he went to his partners and disclosed his feelings about his career and the company. To the chagrin of his partners, he also announced that he was resigning to take a job as an airline mechanic. Ned had truly saved his spirit—and his health.

Just for today, I will ask myself how emotionally honest I am in my work. I will commit to being in touch with my true feelings even if I choose not to express them.

"He that does good for good's sake, seeks neither praise or reward, but he is sure of both in the end."

—William Penn

Most workers have received a bonus in one job or another. Marguerita's company struggled with the idea of giving bonuses, yet they knew their pay scale was at the low end in their field of alcoholism treatment. Several of Marguerita's peers were especially concerned about the cost of bonuses, with heavy payouts to senior employees. Others in the management team also thought that giving annual pay raises and bonuses overindulged people. Although new as human resources director, Marguerita stood her ground. Despite negative reactions from many of her peers, she gave employees bonuses and pay raises as well. But her greatest challenge was satisfying the long-term employees. Through the help of a financial planning firm, Marguerita was able to offer long-term employees individual help with their personal financial planning. This creative strategy not only strengthened the spirits at work, but deepened the respect of her co-workers.

Just for today, I will consider what a bonus would mean to me.

December 8 ⌒ *Reconciliation*

"Out of intense complexities, intense simplicities emerge."

—Winston Churchill

Has unfinished business with someone ever prevented you from being fully present in your work?

When Geoff and Alicia started a new nonprofit center in their community, they worked closely together. Alicia served as the executive director and Geoff, a medical doctor, became the public figure and drew most of the media attention. Alicia did not want to admit that she was jealous of Geoff's youth, his education, and his speaking success. An unspoken tension grew; Alicia made hostile comments about Geoff that spread into the community. Their financial contributors became concerned. Geoff decided to leave the center but first wanted to speak with Alicia about their relationship. Geoff apologized to Alicia for his part in what had gone wrong and assured her that he, too, was disappointed in the tarnishing of their dream. Alicia felt his sincerity and together they reviewed their long history and decided to try again. Geoff and Alicia's reconciliation created a renewed environment in their center.

Just for today, I will ask myself where I might need to reconcile some differences in my world of work. I will recognize that fractures are born, and healed, through relationships.

"One of the truths of our time is the hunger deep in people all over the planet for coming into relationship with each other."

—Mary Caroline Richards

Do you feel a sense of connection through your work? Connection with others helps keep a work system healthy and stimulating.

Mark thought it was unimportant to experience a connection at work; he used to say, "Well, this is only my job, you know!" What Mark did not let others know was that he was shy about meeting new people; it seemed to him that all those around him were extroverts. One day Mark was asked to train Martha, a new, young employee. Although this was not part of his official job duties, Mark felt he could not refuse. Yet he wondered why he was asked to do this task. He did notice that young Martha was also shy. Also like Mark, she was a highly productive accountant. Mark had to take Martha to other departments to train her in their departmental systems. He set up numerous meetings to introduce Martha to department heads. Early into the process, he began to recognize how connected he felt, even in his introversion, with other employees. Through his training work, Mark learned that indeed he was a part of the whole.

Just for today, I will consider how and with whom I feel connected in my work. I know how primary connection is for my life's work.

December 10 ⁓ *Stimulation*

"We have too many people who live without working, and we have altogether too many who work without living."

—Dean Charles R. Brown

How do you find stimulation in your work—just what ignites you?

Gary, a young entrepreneurial president of a small growing technology company, stays stimulated through his creative work in helping declining communities grow through employment. When Gary expands his business into a new market, he knows he is also fulfilling his purpose—to keep a community from going under. He enters small towns hurt by downsizing or dying industries. His approach is to become a friend to the community, not just an employer. Gary's belief in contributing and giving back to society is fulfilled in all his work endeavors; he also helps support the community agencies in the towns he enters. When Gary begins a new community project, he not only brings good to the community but also creates goodwill. This keeps him personally stimulated and helps his spirit soar.

Just for today, I will ask myself what brings me stimulation in my work. I will take the initiative to continue to stay stimulated throughout my life.

"If you want creative workers, give them enough time to play."

Is your workplace playful? When Georgiana began her new job in an ad agency, she was surprised at how dull and flat it felt. When her supervisor, Ted, asked her how she was adjusting, she said, "I don't see any energy around here." Ted was quite surprised at Georgiana's candor, especially as a new employee, yet he knew she was right. Ever since the company had lost its major account, spirits had been low. One day, Georgiana came to work with a camera and took photos of her co-workers making their funniest faces possible. After developing the film, she came in very early one morning and tacked the zany photos all around the office. When people entered work that morning, chuckles and rippling laughter were heard throughout the office. Employees clustered around the displays and immediately wanted to award some zany prizes for the silliest photos. Ted, realizing how long it had been since they had laughter in the office, thanked Georgiana for taking a first step toward restoring spirits.

Just for today, I will ask myself how I can massage my spirit by bringing a sense of playfulness to my work.

December 12 ∿ *Surprise*

"Everything that is new or uncommon raises a pleasure in the imagination, because it fills the soul with an agreeable surprise, gratifies its curiosity, and gives it an idea of which it was not before possessed."

—Joseph Addison

Can you recall when you last had a surprise at work? Surprises can either dampen or ignite our spirits.

Jolene had been an outstanding academic all of her adult life and a quiet contributor to the university in many ways. She was pleased when asked to serve on the search committee for a new university president. As the committee was deep into the process, Jolene excused herself from the meeting one day to go teach a science seminar. As soon as she left, a committee member said, "Well, now that Jolene is out of the room, what about *her* as a candidate?" The group members unanimously agreed to name her as their first choice on their selection list. When Jolene returned for the next meeting, the chair said, "Jolene, we want to thank you for going off to teach your class last week. We made a very important decision in your absence—we want you as university president!" Jolene was stunned, surprised, and elated. With soaring spirits, she humbly accepted the surprise offer.

Just for today, I will consider how I respond to surprises and how I can create a pleasant surprise for someone in my world.

"I simply cannot understand the passion that some people have for making themselves thoroughly uncomfortable and then boasting about it afterward."

—Patricia Moyes

How do you find comfort in your work? We all have ways of experiencing comfort in our daily schedule. Comfort can bring deep satisfaction. It does not always come automatically but often requires effort. Sometimes we find comfort by doing a task that engages our natural talents; it is something we can ease back and lean into.

Ann, a longtime psychologist, spoke about what brought her the greatest comfort during her career: "I guess I would have to say that it is seeing someone I have mentored come along and grow into a successful whole being in their work." She continued, "And perhaps the greatest contribution I have made in my career life has been to mentor seven women Ph.D.s in my field." Ann has been a mature role model for women professionals for many years; exercising her strengths is what brings her comfort.

Just for today, I will ask myself how and where I feel my greatest comfort. I will also seek to provide comfort to others.

December 14 ⌒ *Development*

"The manager maintains; the leader develops."

—Warren Bennis

Have you ever thought about your own development? Or have you considered how you help others develop?

Kevin wasn't aware that he lacked knowledge on development. He had grown up in an era before the term "development plan" was common. He was a kind person and a fair leader, but expected that people would somehow innately have what they needed to go forward in their work. Kevin was quite shocked when four of his younger, most promising employees resigned over an eighteen-month period. At first he attributed it to their competition, but then decided he had better conduct some interviews to see what had happened. He was especially surprised when Jose resigned, his most promising leader who had just received the "Employee of the Year" award. In the interview, Jose said, "Why, I never saw anywhere for me to go here; no one ever spoke to me about where I would or could go or what I would need to develop in me to get there." Unfortunately, it took this hard lesson for Kevin to understand the importance of employee development.

Just for today, I will ask myself how I am contributing to the development of others. My own spiritual development grows as I can help others grow.

"It's not so much how busy you are, but why you are busy. The bee is praised. The mosquito swatted."

—Mary O'Conner

How do you see the results of your work? For an acting company, the results of the long, arduous rehearsals are found in the nightly performances. For people working in business, seeing the results at the end of the month can help sustain the spirit.

Lanette's job involved working with people and hearing their stories. Because of the nature of this work, hard and fast results were not available. She could look at retention figures and annual job satisfaction surveys, but these did not provide her with the sense of satisfaction that she longed for. Realizing she needed to find this fulfillment elsewhere, she enrolled in a cooking class at the local community college. Lanette was excited to have an area in her world that could sustain her need for concrete results. When she had a failed soufflé, it was clear and unambiguous. Realizing that she would never have the concrete results that many have in their work worlds, Lanette found a way to achieve this balance in her life through her new passion—cooking.

Just for today, I will consider how important concrete results are to me. Do I require hard and fast results, or is a general feeling of satisfaction sufficient? I will recognize that I can turn to outside interests to find the type of results I desire.

December 16 ⁓ *Inspiring Others*

"Inspiration may be a form of super-consciousness, or perhaps of subconsciousness—I wouldn't know. But I am sure it is the antithesis of self-consciousness."

—Aaron Copland

Do you know who inspires you? And are you aware of the times you inspire others?

When Lee thought about what ignited her spirit, she said it was bringing a group of people together and leading them to a new way of thinking. The satisfaction of doing so is especially evident to Lee in her volunteer work, which she spends about 20 percent of her time doing. When she set out to organize a group of mental health professionals in her state, she faced a real struggle in the early days. Yes, the professionals wanted licensure for insurance coverage for the people they served (many of whom are from low-income families), but many of her cohorts were highly suspicious of any legislative process. They simply did not trust politicians. With Lee leading the initiative for more than two years, the group finally received licensure coverage so that they, too, could be treated like the professionals they truly are. Lee's high energy inspired the spirit in others.

Just for today, I will ask myself how I inspire others and how I contribute to the inspirational dimension in my workplace.

"Do all the good you can. By all the means you can. In all the ways you can. In all the places you can. At all the times you can. To all the people you can. As long as ever you can."

—John Wesley

How do you reach out to others? Or do you expect others to come to you?

Nancy worked as a middle manager in a large corporation that frequently received requests for help. After a fifteen-year career, Nancy quit her job to do something drastically different. She decided to reach out to people in her community. She lived in an area with a high number of immigrant families, pregnant teens, and school dropouts. While there was illiteracy, Nancy found the real problem was that people didn't know how to access community programs that were designed to help them. She coordinated an information center, worked with local schools and community colleges to set up mentoring programs for troubled teens, and opened a school program for unwed mothers. Nancy was not very concerned about the mistakes people made in the past; she was deeply concerned about their futures and who they could become. In a short time, she had students helping others, many tutoring younger, at-risk children. The community's dropout rate decreased within one year. Nancy had enlivened her spirit by reaching out.

Just for today, I will reach out in some way to another person. I know that my spirit receives through giving.

December 18 ⟡ *Extra Steps*

"It is normal to give away a little of one's life in order not to lose it all."

—Albert Camus

How often have you taken that extra step to make a difference in someone's life?

Last year when trekking in Tibet with wilderness guide Gary McCue, I saw remarkable examples of quiet extra stepping. As Gary led our group high into the Himalayas surrounding Lhasa, the capital of Tibet, we became weary in the early afternoons on the high slopes and needed to rest often. Yet one day Gary said, "Why, I thought we could just visit the monks up in their cave homes and that you might enjoy a cup of tea up there." We looked up and, seeing the steep trails up the mountainside, heaved deep sighs. Our spirits wanted to proceed, but our bodies spoke to us of tiredness. As we much later entered the dwelling of one of the monks, Gary pulled out a sack he had carried with him. In it he had eye drops for the old monk who had a serious eye disease. Gary had said nothing to us about his purpose in wanting to visit the monk; he simply took the extra steps to bring relief to another human being, a loving model for us all.

Just for today, I will silently take some extra steps to make someone else's day a little brighter.

Ingenuity ⌒ December 19

"They can, because they think they can."

—Author unknown

How would you describe your most ingenious act? It may have been an idea contributed at a meeting or a new method for making work more efficient. Many of us have known ingenious moments in our work lives, yet have not named them.

When Dravid first came to the United States, he opened retail stores one at a time, as his father had done in India. Then he studied computer science in night school and became very excited about creating a marketplace on the Internet. Within a year, he announced his Internet free–greeting card company. Yet Dravid did not care about greeting cards; this was simply his way of attracting customers. He knew that once he had the clientele, he could offer almost anything. Within another year, he had hundreds of thousands of strikes from possible customers; now he began selling the books and books on tape he had longed to market. It was not long before the major "banner advertisers" courted him for his highly productive marketplace. Dravid's ingenuity fed his spirit.

Just for today, I will assess what part ingenuity has played in my life. I will also consider how ingenious acts can keep my spirit alive.

December 20 ～ *Self-Protection*

"Don't play fair in an unfair game."

—Anonymous

Have you ever been punished for something that happened at work?

Ruth tightened when she received a feedback form from her boss, Ben, inviting open and candid opinions about his leadership. He would address the feedback at an upcoming retreat. She did not want to be punished for providing honest feedback, and she did not trust him. Ben had a reputation for punishing people who challenged him. Ruth also knew that Ben felt very competitive with her recent success. Others who had confronted him had been demoted in the guise of "restructuring." Ruth had to make a decision. Her spirit demanded truth, and her survival demanded politics. Ruth made a conscious choice: she filled out a "careful" survey that she gave to Ben and then filled one out honestly for her files. She felt in this way she could honor her spirit, her truth.

Just for today, I will be aware of my possible naïveté and know when I don't feel safe. By trusting my intuition and my experience, I will honor my spirit.

"We change lives."

—Santa Fe Mountain Center

Have you ever viewed the work you do as healing work? People heal in a variety of ways.

Sky Gray, the director of the Santa Fe Mountain Center and a leader in experiential education, organizes therapeutic adventure programs for at-risk groups in New Mexico; the goal of the programs is to promote personal change. One of the center's programs takes HIV/AIDS patients into the wilderness; the group also works with troubled juvenile offenders as well as victims of sexual abuse. All of their work centers on healing broken spirits. They have been widely recognized for the Native Emergence program that emphasizes building confidence in American Indian youth dealing with transition between life on a reservation or pueblo and the public school system. Many of the activities focus on utilizing problem-solving skills, risking, teamwork, and appropriate communication. One of their newest programs is "Climbing Up, Climbing Out," an adventure-based empowerment program for gay, lesbian, bisexual, transgendered youth. Sky Gray and her fine staff truly ignite spirits while contributing to the greater community.

Just for today, I will consider how my work can help heal. I will work toward helping people in need, knowing that such work strengthens my spirit.

December 22 〜 *Generosity*

"There is no delight in owning anything unshared."

—Lucius Annaeus Seneca

How have you known generosity at work? Do you work in a generous environment?

Jill worked for a firm that was incredibly generous, but one day Will, the company's owner, took the grand prize. Jill knew that a division of the company was to be sold. Will had called an all-company meeting to announce the sale and also to reassure the employees that their jobs were secure. He spent almost half an hour recognizing the contributions of all those who had helped make the sale happen. But the biggest surprise came the next morning when employees entered the office and found a company e-mail awaiting them. It was a message of congratulations for their generosity in helping the company grow to this point. Will said he wanted to share some of the profits from the sale, and for each year of their service, employees would receive a five-hundred-dollar bonus.

Just for today, I will ask how I am generous with others in words and in actions.

"You will recognize your own path when you come upon it, because you will suddenly have all the energy and imagination you will ever need."

—Jerry Gillies

Do you feel as if you've been following your true pathway? Sometimes it takes years before we even ask ourselves that question.

Mike had been a dentist for almost twenty years and was becoming terribly bored. Even teaching dentistry at the university no longer stimulated him. He began to take courses in the healing arts, studying Chinese medicine, massage, and other alternative healing methods. He volunteered to assist in personal growth seminars; he also read extensively in the field and met an entirely new group of people. Within a few years, he took the risk: he scaled down his schedule to only part time and then finally left his profession. Mike had never been so happy in his life; he had found his true pathway. Still he struggled with the transition for a few years but knew that if "friends" could not respect his choices, he must let go. A few good friends did support him through his transition; Mike then developed seminars to help others find their true pathways.

Just for today, I will ask whether I am on my true pathway. I will be rigorously honest with myself about how much satisfaction and joy I bring to my spirit.

December 24 ～ *Firm Caring*

"Good, the more communicated, more abundant grows."

—John Milton

Do you sometimes have to exercise firm caring? *Firm caring* means taking a firm stand with someone and doing it with good heart.

Some time ago I met a seventeen-year-old boy in East Africa who was as manipulative as he was high spirited. His work was to beg or to con. His greeting to us was, "Pen, Madam? Pen?" followed by, "You bring me money?" We smiled, while saying, "We bring you friendship." He continued with repeating his lines; we continued responding, "We bring you friendship." Later in our trip, we were rushing to the airport to catch our flight home. Confused about which bus to take to the airport, we frantically asked in halting Swahili, and in English, to get information. If late, we would miss our connection. Suddenly, the young man appeared. He quickly directed us to the appropriate bus and told us what money to use. When we offered to give him something for his help, he smiled widely and said, "You brought me friendship, Madam. . . . I bring you friendship."

Just for today, I will explore where I should take stands of firm caring and recognize that the reward may not be immediate but indeed will come.

Believing ∼ December 25

"To accomplish great things we must not only act, but also dream, not only plan, but also believe."

—Anatole France

Have you ever experienced success in your work, knowing that your believing made it happen?

When Sabriye Tenberken became blind, she was determined to learn Braille and become educated about blindness. When studying Tibetology at the University of Bonn, she learned about the blind children of Tibet. She learned that the region had a high rate of blind children due to high altitude and sun rays, lack of vitamin A, and heating with yak dung. Sabriye visited Tibetan villages. She believed that she could develop programs to educate and rehabilitate the children who were shunned because of their Tibetan heritage and their blindness. The blind Sabriye developed a Tibetan script, or alphabet, for the blind. Because of the Chinese occupation of Tibet, she decided the children needed to learn Chinese as well. Today the children of the Project for the Blind in Tibet are being educated. One woman's beliefs had made miracles happen.

Just for today, I will consider how I can act on my beliefs to make a difference.

December 26 〜 Investment

"Begin to make the kind of investment of personal time which will assure that those who come after us will live as well."

—Charles W. Bray III

What kind of an investment have you made in your work? Thad and his brothers, David and Mike, have invested all of their energy into their adventure travel company. Their company is based on their philosophy that our natural environments are intimately and irrevocably linked to people, locally and globally. Their investment in East African lands and people has been constant. The company leads walking safaris through Masai land and pays the villagers just as they do game parks so that the Masai people can also earn revenue for their land's recreational use. They have invested in communities by forming partnerships with local villages. Through the nonprofit fund, they establish partnerships to empower communities to manage the health of their natural resources, including wildlife and wilderness. They have also invested in educational programs for children and have supported individuals, particularly women. Their investment in East Africa has brought dividends of new schools where children are educated.

Just for today, I will assess what my major investments are in my work and what kind of dividends (tangible and intangible) I reap from them.

Natural Capitalism ~ December 27

"What does this place require us to do? What will it allow us to do? What will it help us to do?"

—Wendell Berry

Have you ever considered what your workplace would look like if it centered its principles for operating on the next industrial revolution, the natural capitalism movement? Natural capitalism is the focus of a book by Paul Hawken and proposes a paradigm shift from thinking of selling goods like lightbulbs, for instance, to providing illumination. This movement, which is becoming increasingly popular, promotes lucrative businesses that are environmentally sensitive. There are many examples of natural capitalism today. One is in Santa Fe at the Inn of the Anasazi Hotel. In the hotel, the art comes from local artists; the toiletries are made from traditional Native American medicinal herbs; and the furniture, crafted by local artisans, is produced from local resources. The gourmet restaurant buys 90 percent of its ingredients from local organic farmers. The staff are paid two hours a week to volunteer for local groups. Staff turnover is low; occupancy rates at the hotel are high. Many of us have heard about the "spirit in the earth." The Inn of the Anasazi is fanning that spirit.

Just for today, I will ask myself how I can contribute to natural capitalism and find ways of integrating natural resources into my work.

December 28 ∽ *Love*

"Love is a choice. . . . a willingness to be present to others without pretense or guile."

—Carter Heyward

How have you known love in work? *Love* is not a word we typically think of at work, unless it is someone's romantic love affair. Yet we know many people who would say they love their work. Others feel a true sense of loving in their workplaces. In fact, some studies have shown that many people prefer to spend time in their offices rather than their homes because they are treated so well, so respectfully, at work. Love has many dimensions when put in the context of work.

The other day I asked a friend about her new job. She replied that she felt good about the people with whom she worked. She said, "Well, we really get along. . . . We really love each other." She then hurried to say, "Gosh, I mean, well, uh, I guess we really do. . . . We just love each other and treat one another that way." As more people are learning to know love at work, perhaps there will be less blushing about such a wonderful gift to the spirit.

Just for today, I will allow myself to be loving and to accept love at work.

"Giving is the secret of a healthy life. Not necessarily money, but whatever a man (or woman) has of encouragement and sympathy and understanding."

—John D. Rockefeller Jr.

How do you encourage others? And how do you receive encouragement?

Betsy was good at encouraging others. Successful in her law firm, she was also respected in her community and admired by younger people. She was thriving when she learned she had a serious illness. Betsy's life changed overnight: she could no longer maintain an active lifestyle, and travel was restricted. Her doctor predicted that she would be in this state for a few years. Betsy, the optimist and encourager of others, now had to find a way to encourage herself. She had read that about one-fourth of those with her arthritis condition became depressed. Betsy realized her challenge in learning how to encourage herself. She began to interview others with the same diagnosis and read books about living with chronic illness. She started meditating and took some breathing classes. What finally helped Betsy was a journal in which she wrote words of encouragement daily. Although Betsy was forced to endure dramatic lifestyle changes, her encouraging words sustained her spirit.

Just for today, I will focus on encouraging others and recognize that there may come times when I need to encourage myself.

December 30 〜 Dedication

"We will be remembered not for the power of our weapons but for the power of our compassion, and dedication to human welfare."

—Hubert Humphrey

Are you dedicated to making a difference in your work? Rochelle has received numerous awards for her dedication to her work in real estate, not just for her volume of sales, but also for her professionalism. Rochelle does not just sell houses; she sells homes. She considers one's home to be a special place—a sanctuary. Rochelle is dedicated to her mission of finding the best home for the buyer. She also refuses to show people homes out of their price range, knowing the stress that can add. Because of her personal and professional honesty, she will not misrepresent any house. Because of her dedication and commitment to quality, Rochelle has become the most desired Realtor in a major metropolitan area. Rochelle says that her truest form of pay is the satisfaction of her clients who have found their homes.

Just for today, I will ask myself how my dedication plays out in my work. Can I feel a sense of rich satisfaction from my dedication?

"Whether we name the divine presence synchronicity, serendipity, or graced moment matters little. What matters is the reality that our hearts have been understood. Nothing is as real as a healthy dose of magic which restores our spirits."

—Nancy Long

Have you ever known someone who had a spiritual breakthrough at work? Perhaps it was you! Many people would say this is not possible; I know it is.

When Taylor's team decided to have a two-day retreat to work on business planning, they went to an off-site retreat center and participated in a variety of experiential exercises before returning to their retreat work. The outdoor rope course left several team members feeling very vulnerable. Two people then disclosed childhood fears and how frightened they were about going into the wilderness alone for the evening; they asked for support. The group had never known this level of sharing before. By the end of the evening, the team members sat with their arms around one another. They then discussed their personal beliefs about spirituality and how if affected their work. As the group members opened their hearts and expressed how they cared for one another, they experienced a spiritual breakthrough—an opening to their spirits growing at work.

Just for today, I will consider spiritual breakthroughs I have experienced at work and what I did to develop my spirit in other areas of my life.

Index

About the Author

MARILYN MASON, PH.D., is a corporate psychologist, management consultant, speaker, and author who specializes in leadership development, executive coaching, and family business/foundation consulting. A former faculty member at the University of Minnesota, Mason brings her background in communications and family systems into corporate and organizational consulting. Author of *Facing Shame, Making Our Lives Our Own,* and *Seven Mountains: Life Lessons from a Climber's Journal,* Mason lives in Santa Fe, New Mexico.

To find out more about Marilyn Mason or to contact her, visit her Web site at www.marilynmason.com.